Letort Paper

THE MILITARY'S ROLE IN COUNTERTERRORISM: EXAMPLES AND IMPLICATIONS FOR LIBERAL DEMOCRACIES

Geraint Hughes

May 2011

*****

Comments pertaining to this report are invited and should be forwarded to: Director, Strategic Studies Institute, U.S. Army War College, 632 Wright Ave, Carlisle, PA 17013-5046.

*****

The author owes his thanks for critical input from and conversations with colleagues within the Defence Studies Department (DSD) of King's College London, in particular Drs. Tim Bird, Huw Bennett, Katherine Brown, Warren Chin, Tracey German, Jon Hill, Bill Park, Kenneth Payne, Patrick Porter, Christian Tripodi, and Rachel Vincent. He has also derived immense benefit from the staff and students at the Joint Services Command and Staff College (JSCSC), both from the British armed forces and from several foreign services with whom he has had the pleasure of teaching and working with over the past 5 years.

The Military's Role in Counterterrorism has been written for both a professional military and a nonspecialist civilian readership. Readers should note that with certain languages (such as Arabic and Urdu), there is no standard method of transliteration into English. The author's rendition of certain names and phrases therefore may not match those employed by his sources (for example, the author uses "al-Qaeda" rather than "al-Qaida," and "Qasab" rather than "Kasab"). All material cited in this paper is in the public domain, and any factual errors in the text that have escaped the author's attention are his own responsibility.

This Letort Paper is humbly dedicated to the memory of all Coalition military and civil affairs personnel killed on operations in Afghanistan since October 2001.

*****

*****

The Strategic Studies Institute publishes a monthly e-mail newsletter to update the national security community on the research of our analysts, recent and forthcoming publications, and upcoming conferences sponsored by the Institute. Each newsletter also provides a strategic commentary by one of our research analysts. If you are interested in receiving this newsletter, please subscribe on the SSI website at *www.StrategicStudiesInstitute. army.mil/newsletter/*.

ISBN 1-58487-489-9

CONTENTS

FOREWORD

On the morning of September 11, 2001 (9/11), al-Qaeda terrorists hijacked four passenger aircraft, crashing three of them into the World Trade Center in New York City and the Pentagon in Washington, DC, killing up to 3,000 people in the process. Just under 3 years later, a group of predominantly Chechen gunmen took over School Number One in Beslan, North Ossetia, beginning a siege that ended with the death of nearly 400, including 156 children. On the evening of November 26, 2008, 10 members of Lashkar-e-Toiba (LET) began a series of bomb and gun attacks in the Indian city of Mumbai, killing more than 170 people over a 48-hour period. For Americans, Russians, and Indians, each of these attacks was warlike in its proportions and, after each, popular and political opinion demanded a militarized response.

Dr. Geraint Hughes's Letort Paper reminds us that in repeated cases in which liberal democratic states have used their armed forces to fight terrorism--notably Israel against successive Palestinian groups, Britain in Northern Ireland from 1969-98, or indeed America and its allies against al-Qaeda and affiliated groups currently--the employment of military means in counterterrorism has been inherently controversial. As Audrey Kurth Cronin notes, terrorism picks at the vulnerable seam between domestic law and foreign war, and conceptually it does not fit the paradigms of either criminality or warfare.[1] Although a particular state or a coalition of powers may use its militaries to protect its citizens in counterterrorist campaigns, the threat posed by specific terrorist groups has to be treated *sui generis*, and the applicability of military means in counterterrorism depends on a series of factors--these include whether the terrorist threat is a domestic or an international one, the lethality of the groups concerned, and the threat they pose to state stability. Furthermore, the involvement of armed forces in counterterrorism can be problematic. One has only to look at the post-2001 "War on Terror" and the criticisms expressed by foreign governments, members of Congress, human rights activists, journalists, and academics regarding the treatment of detainees at Guantanamo Bay, Cuba; the use of unmanned aerial vehicles (UAVs) in air-strikes in Pakistan; and the civilian casualties caused by U.S. and North Atlantic Treaty Organization (NATO) military operations in Afghanistan.

Dr. Hughes examines the challenges of deploying the military in counterterrorism from both a historical and a contemporary perspective, outlining not only the specific roles that armed forces can perform either to prevent terrorist attacks or to mitigate their consequences, but also the strategic, constitutional, practical, diplomatic, and ethical problems that have arisen from a variety of counterterrorist campaigns, be they in Palestine, Northern Ireland, Quebec, Kashmir, Afghanistan, Pakistan, or the North Caucasus. Clausewitz reminds us that in "war everything is simple, but the simplest thing is difficult,"[2] and this observation is as true of counterterrorism as it is of interstate warfare. For example, the British Army interned Republican terrorist suspects in Northern Ireland from 1971-75, gaining valuable intelligence about the United Kingdom's (UK) adversaries, but this policy also enraged the Catholic community and poisoned relations between the UK and the Republic of Ireland. The Israeli Defense Force (IDF) has used targeted killings against the leaderships of *Fatah*, *Hamas*, and *Hezbollah*, but has been unable to translate tactical-level successes into outcomes that serve Israel's overall strategic objective, which is a regional peace settlement that gives the Jewish state recognition and security from its neighbors.

As is the case with other democracies, America's Soldiers, Sailors, Airmen and Marines are trained in the application of controlled and discriminate violence. Current operations in Iraq and Afghanistan have demonstrated repeatedly that whenever the U.S. military confronts irregular adversaries that conceal themselves within a civilian population, it is both ethically important and strategically sound to employ force with precision, and in such a manner as to minimize casualties among the wider populace. Members of the armed forces are also required to be accountable for their actions and to ensure that their operations are coordinated with those of civilian governmental agencies, host nation officials, and other allied powers. The challenges posed by the current "Long War" are many and, as Hughes observes, Western civilian and military officials have the hard task of resolving the dilemma facing all democratic states confronted by terrorism; namely, how they fight this threat and protect their citizens without undermining the constitutional, legal, and normative characteristics upon which government by consent is founded. In this respect, this paper is required reading for military practitioners and scholars who wish to develop an informed understanding of the complexities of counterterrorism, which will be a source of considerable deliberation within our defense establishment and those of allied countries for the foreseeable future.

Douglas C. Lovelace

DOUGLAS C. LOVELACE, JR.
Director
Strategic Studies Institute

ENDNOTES - FOREWORD

1. Audrey Kurth Cronin, *How Terrorism Ends: Understanding the Decline and Demise of Terrorist Campaigns*, Princeton NJ: Princeton University Press, 2009, p. 116.

2. Carl von Clausewitz, *On War*, Michael Howard and Peter Paret, eds. and trans., Princeton, NJ: Princeton University Press, 1984, p. 119.

ABOUT THE AUTHOR

GERAINT HUGHES is a lecturer with the Defence Studies Department, King's College London, and has taught at the Joint Services Command and Staff College, Shrivenham, United Kingdom, since July 2005. He served with the Territorial Army between June 1999 and April 2005, and was deployed on an operational tour with British forces in Southeastern Iraq between May and November 2004. His research interests include contemporary land warfare, the use of the military in counterterrorism and counterinsurgency, and proxy war. His second book, *My Enemy's Enemy: Proxy Warfare in International Politics*, is due to be published by Sussex Academic Press in 2012.

SUMMARY

In the aftermath of the September 11, 2001 (9/11) attacks, the U.S. Government was criticized for adopting a militaristic response to the threat posed by al-Qaeda and affiliated groups. As the Israeli-Palestinian conflict and that in Northern Ireland demonstrate, any liberal democracy that uses its armed forces to combat terrorism will incur controversy both domestically and internationally. The use of military power in counterterrorism is contentious, because historical and contemporary examples suggest that it can have the following negative strategic, political, and ethical effects: The state can generate indigenous resentment that terrorist groups can exploit, and can, by resorting to military force, kill or maim a substantial number of civilians. It can also encourage human rights abuses that are antithetical to the norms of a liberal democracy--such as the maltreatment and torture of detainees --and can (as demonstrated by Uruguay in 1973 and Russia currently) lead to the subversion of the constitutional order and its replacement by authoritarian rule.

While addressing these criticisms, this Letort Paper also argues that there are contingencies in which democratic states are obliged to employ military means in order to protect their citizens from the threat of terrorism, whether in a purely domestic context or when facing a transnational terrorist network such as al-Qaeda. While outlining the specific roles that armed forces can perform (including hostage rescue, military aid to the civil authority, interdiction, and intelligence-gathering), this paper also describes the strategic, political, diplomatic, and ethical challenges that arise from using military means to fight terrorism either on one's home soil or in the international arena. This paper's principal conclusion is that democratic governments can use their armed forces if the existing police/judicial framework cannot address the threat posed by terrorists, but that military means have to be integrated as part of an overarching strategy to contain terrorism and to limit the capacity of its practitioners to conduct attacks against citizens. The author also outlines a series of questions that civilian decisionmakers should ideally resolve prior to turning counterterrorism missions over to their military counterparts.

MAPS

The four maps are provided courtesy of the University Libraries of the University of Texas, Austin, Texas. The photograph comes from the author's own collection.

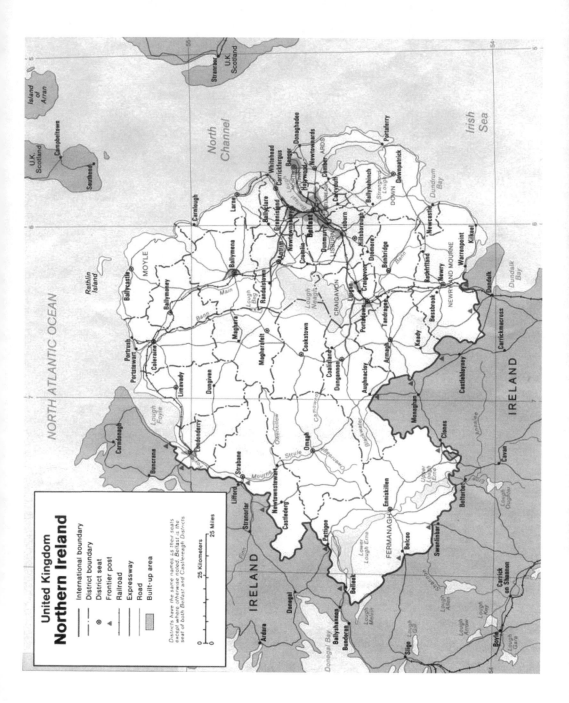

Map 1. Northern Ireland.

Map 2. Chechnya and Neighboring Russian
Republics.

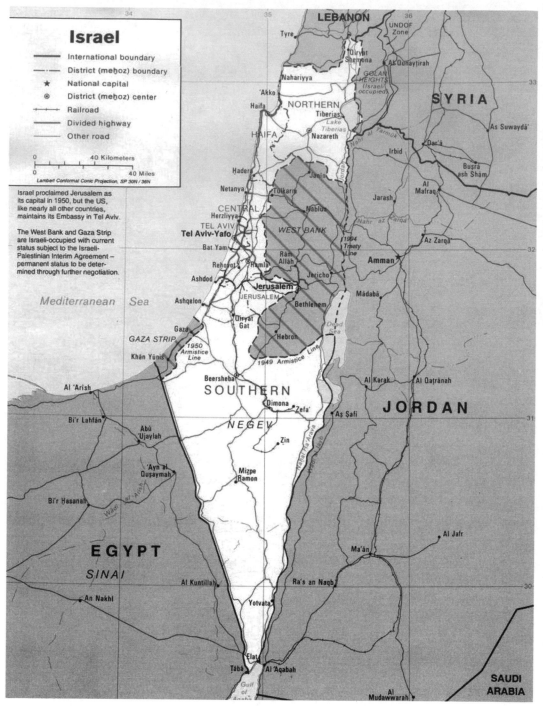

Map 3. Israel, the Gaza Strip, and the West Bank.

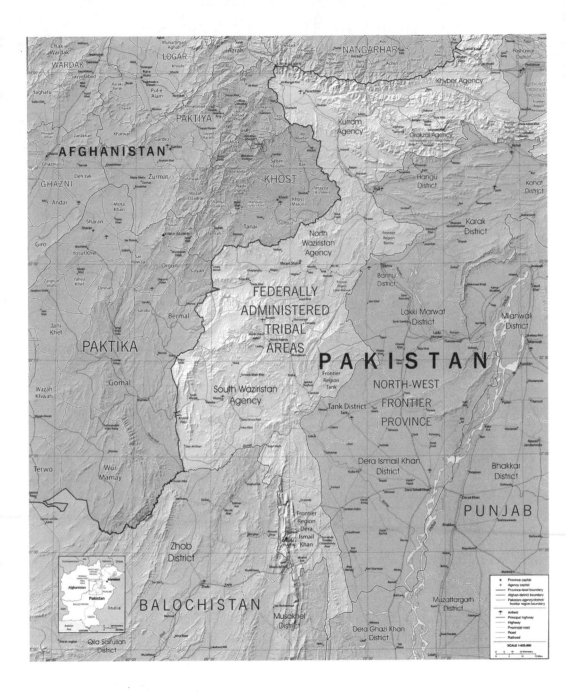

Map 4. The FATA, Pakistan.

THE MILITARY'S ROLE IN COUNTERTERRORISM: EXAMPLES AND IMPLICATIONS FOR LIBERAL DEMOCRACIES

INTRODUCTION

During an official visit to Mumbai, India, on January 15, 2009, British Foreign Secretary David Miliband delivered a speech which essentially condemned the counterterrorism policy the United States had adopted in the aftermath of al-Qaeda's attacks on New York City and Washington, DC, on September 11, 2001 (9/11). Miliband declared that "[the] belief that the correct response to the terrorist threat was a military one: to track down and kill a hardcore of extremists" was "misleading and mistaken," and his criticisms reflected the widespread view of the Western center-left that the War on Terror declared by former President George W. Bush had been entirely counter-productive.[1] Domestic political opponents accused the then-Foreign Secretary of cowardice and opportunism; Miliband did, after all, have plenty of opportunities to publicly express his concerns about American counterterrorist policy well before the end of the Bush administration's tenure in office. Yet the majority of critics missed the key flaw in his speech, namely the stark contrast between his comments and the venue chosen for their delivery, the Taj Mahal hotel.[2]

This hotel was one of the five targets selected by the 10 heavily-armed Pakistani terrorists from *Lashkar e-Toiba* (LET) who conducted a sea-borne assault on Mumbai on November 26, 2008. The Taj Mahal, like the Trident Oberoi and the Leopold Café, had been chosen by LET (a jihadi group originally set up by the Pakistani Army to fight as insurgents in Kashmir) because they were patronized by Western tourists. But the attackers also chose Nariman House (a cultural center for the city's Jewish community) and the Chhatrapati Shivaji train station, where many of their victims were commuters returning home from work. Over the course of 3 days, the LET terrorists killed over 170 people in a series of grenade and gun attacks at these locations, causing pandemonium and overwhelming the inadequately-armed and poorly-trained police. As one group of analysts noted after the event, the civil authorities in Mumbai were simply unable to cope with a terrorist atrocity that was un-precedented in scale and scope:

> [The LET raid] was sequential and highly mobile. Multiple teams attacked several locations at once—

2

combining armed assaults, carjackings, drive-by shootings, prefabricated IEDs [Improvised Explosive Devices], targeted killings (of policemen and selected foreigners), building takeovers, and barricade and hostage situations.[3]

All these tactics had been implemented in previous terrorist attacks; what was unique in this instance was their combination. From November 26-29, Mumbai was essentially subjected to a commando raid, albeit one directed against civilian rather than military targets, and it required the intervention of the Indian Army and Special Forces to quell the LET attackers. Miliband not only demonstrated questionable judgment in choosing the Taj Mahal as the venue for his homily, but the reality of what had happened at the hotel — not to mention the city as a whole — suggested that there would be circumstances in which states would have no option but to adopt a military response to terrorism.[4]

Furthermore, Miliband's implicit expectation that the new U.S. President would repudiate his predecessor's apparently discredited policies were disabused by the continuation of the Predator Unmanned Aerial Vehicle (UAV) strikes into the Federally Administered Tribal Areas (FATA) of Northwest Pakistan, and also by President Barack Obama's speech on U.S. policy toward Afghanistan and Pakistan on March 27, 2009. Although President Obama avoided the contentious phrase "War on Terror," the substance of his speech differed little from those made by his predecessor. He asserted that a U.S.-North Atlantic Treaty Organization (NATO) victory in Afghanistan was essential to defeat the radical Islamist ideology that inspired al-Qaeda, and to forestall any future mass casualty atrocities by its adherents. Furthermore, although Obama outlined a policy of fostering socioeconomic development to remove the causes of internal strife in both Afghanistan and Pakistan, he still emphasized the military contribution to stabilizing both countries, stressing that "we will use all elements of our national power to *defeat al-Qaeda* and to defend America, our allies, and all who seek a better future."[5] The following November, Secretary of State Hillary Clinton expressed the U.S. objective in Afghanistan, which was to "dismantle, *eradicate and defeat* those who attacked us [on 9/11]."[6] President Obama reiterated his aim of defeating al-Qaeda in late-March 2010 while addressing U.S. troops in Afghanistan, and the following month he announced that the Central Intelligence Agency (CIA) and the U.S. military had received his authorization to kill Anwar al-Awlaki, an American-born radical cleric thought to be hiding in Yemen.[7] Counterterrorism is therefore as much a priority for the current U.S. administration as it was for its Republican predecessors, and has retained its military aspect. According to press reports, Obama has opted to bolster the parts of the U.S. defense budget that are of direct relevance to the Long War (notably the budget for U.S. Special Operations Command—increasing it from $9bn in 2010 to $9.8bn in 2011—and assistance to foreign militaries, raised from $350m in 2010 to $500m in 2011).[8]

On the other side of the Atlantic, Miliband's own colleague—then-Defence Secretary John Hutton—further undermined his arguments in a speech in late-April 2009, which advocated a "rebalancing of investment [within the United Kingdom's (UK) armed forces] in technology, equipment and people to meet the challenge of irregular warfare," notably terrorism, and increased attention to Special Forces and other assets that could be employed in this task.[9] Although it remains to be seen whether this aspect of Labour policy will influence the forthcoming Strategic Defence and Security Review (SDSR) initiated by its Conservative-Liberal coalition successor, it is evident that both the U.S. and British governments still consider that counterterrorist policy requires a significant military input.[10]

The decade since 9/11 has seen a prolonged debate within the Western world—incorporating politicians, the professional military, academics, and the media—concerning what British political scientist Norman Geras wryly refers to as FKATWOT ("Formerly Known as the War on Terror").[11] The revulsion shown by critics toward the essential idea of a war against terrorism is understandable, given the manner in which the Bush administration (with British compliance) used 9/11 as one of the pretexts for the invasion of Saddam Hussein's Iraq, not to mention revelations about the treatment of suspected terrorists held in Guantanamo Bay, Cuba, and CIA black prisons, in addition to those delivered by extraordinary rendition to Middle Eastern countries where the local security forces systematically torture prisoners.[12] Furthermore, the policies of the Bush administration (in addition to those associated with former British Prime Minister Tony Blair) have both antagonized Muslim opinion worldwide and raised concerns about the state of civil liberties in both the United States and the United Kingdom (UK).[13]

As Ahmed Rashid has rightly pointed out, U.S. declarations of counterterrorist policy placed insufficient emphasis on the need for other policies to fight Islamic extremism. These included the requirement for political, economic, and social reforms within Pakistan, Uzbekistan, Yemen, and other countries where al-Qaeda has associated itself with local Islamist militants.[14] David Kilcullen also notes that the Bush administration's extravagant rhetoric inherently associated al-Qaeda with other Islamist groups such as Hezbollah and Hamas, thereby not only embroiling the United States in a protracted conflict with a multitude of foes (including many not actually aligned with Osama bin Laden), but also contributing to al-Qaeda's propaganda claim that the War on Terror was in fact a war against Islam. In this respect, Obama's conciliatory speech at Cairo University on June 4, 2009, was intended to repair some of the damage done to the U.S. reputation within the Muslim world by the previous administration's rhetoric and policies.[15]

These are all pertinent criticisms of the direction of American (and allied) counterterrorist policies since 2001, but there are also journalists and scholars who argue that *all* military responses to terrorism are inherently illegitimate and conceptually flawed.[16] Take George Kassimeris's statement that "[the] real War on Terror ought to be fought by means of effective police work and intelligence and a genuine hearts and minds campaign to separate the terrorists from the communities where they derive their support."[17] This is undoubtedly the ideal, and it certainly represents the model applied by West European governments combating domestic extremism. However, policing, public relations, and community outreach could not address the problem posed by al-Qaeda's symbiotic relationship with Taliban-ruled Afghanistan from 1996 to 2001. The idea that post-9/11 Osama bin Laden and the thousands of well-armed and trained fighters under his command could have been quashed without resort to military force is absurd, given that diplomatic efforts to persuade the Taliban regime to expel al-Qaeda and cease providing it with a sanctuary had all come to naught. After Mumbai, it is also clear that when a small, indoctrinated, and well-armed group is able to infiltrate a major city and launch lethal attacks against its citizens, normal policing measures simply do not work. Both these cases show that there may be contingencies in which a government (or governments) has no choice but to involve armed forces in the defense of states and their societies against a terrorist organization, and to argue otherwise is to argue in the face of reality.[18]

The employment of the military in counterterrorism has been examined before, but this subject requires a more up-to-date analysis.[19] In order to begin to comprehend this issue, scholars need to understand the historical background as well as the challenges posed by contemporary counterterrorism. Any analysis of this subject is complicated by the fact that terrorism often co-exists with other forms of internal conflict, and in practice it is often difficult to distinguish between counterterrorism and counterinsurgency (COIN). Furthermore, terrorism can also be a by-product of intense civil strife, as was the case with Lebanon between 1975 and 1990, and Somalia currently.[20]

The confusion between insurgency and terrorism is not helped by willful acts of conflation, such as the Bush administration's insistence that the invasion and occupation of Iraq was part of the War on Terror.[21] It is for this reason that, aside from specific examples which may be relevant in future contingencies, this paper will not cover the consequences of Operation IRAQI FREEDOM, or the course of U.S. and Coalition operations in Iraq since the spring of 2003. The author also does not discuss the war in Afghanistan in any great detail, except with reference to specific aspects of Operation EDURING FREEDOM that are relevant to the debate about military contributions to counterterrorism. A prime example (covered in the concluding chapter) is the debate within the Obama administration as to whether the U.S. military can reduce its commitment from the current COIN campaign in Afghanistan to a more restrictive focus, using UAVs, Special Forces, and indigenous tribal allies to cripple al-Qaeda and to eradicate its operatives.[22]

Readers also need to bear in mind the historical trends that have shaped terrorism as an international phenomenon over the past 50 years. These include decolonization, the end of the Cold War, the process of democratization (most notably in Eastern Europe, the former Union of Soviet Socialist Republics [USSR], Turkey, Pakistan, Indonesia, and Latin America), and also the transition from old to new terrorism. The latter is a particularly worrying trend for those scholars and policymakers who grew accustomed to the idea that the violence inflicted by terrorists was limited by the latter's overall objectives, and whose experiences were shaped by an era in which the Enniskillen and Omagh bombings in Northern Ireland (1987 and 1998, respectively) could be classified as mass casualty attacks. Recent experience—notably that of Chechnya— shows that terrorism can also have a negative effect on the process of democratization, retarding political reform and ultimately assisting the return of authoritarianism, as has been evident in Russia under former President, and current Prime Minister Vladimir Putin.[23]

As far as research methodology is concerned, there are limitations in the prevailing metrics-based approach employed by political scientists. The accumulation of data sets and their statistical analysis take scholars only so far, and run a clear risk of sacrificing contextual understanding for reductionist assessments. In certain cases, verifiable data are a rare commodity; readers will see this for themselves in the third section, with reference to the varying estimates on the number of al-Qaeda and Taliban militants accounted for by Predator strikes in the FATA. One of the principal points of this paper is that the use of military force can only be envisaged in given circumstances, and that in adverse political and social conditions it can have a deleterious effect. For example, it is commonly believed that for the government side to win a counterterrorist campaign its security forces must outnumber its adversary by at least 10:1. Kilcullen reminds us that during the Cyprus emergency of 1955-59, the British Army outnumbered the Ethniki Organosi Kyprion Agoniston (EOKA) by 110:1. Yet the latter won, largely because it gained the passive support of the Greek Cypriot majority, and also because the British government lacked the will to conduct a campaign of unrestricted repression against the civilian populace, given domestic and international pressure in favor of self-determination and independence from colonial rule. The Cyprus example shows that if scholars and practitioners studying terrorism are to use history as an educational tool, they will need to understand the varying factors and developments that made the difference between the successful use of military means and failure.[24]

This paper will therefore address both the potential utility and the pitfalls of employing armed forces in counterterrorist roles, taking recent historical and contemporary examples from liberal democratic states (mainly, but not exclusively, the United States and UK), and also democratizing ones (notably the Russian Federation and Turkey). This is not to say that nondemocratic states can offer no useful examples for counterterrorism as a whole. For example, the Saudi authorities have attracted favorable attention for their deradicalization program, in which imams de-indoctrinate imprisoned jihadis prior to their release and reintegration into society.[25] However, the military record of nondemocratic states fighting terrorism is invariably a dismal one. The mailed-fist approach that characterized President Islam Karimov's fight against the Islamic Movement of Uzbekistan (IMU) since the mid-1990s has only inspired further support for Islamism in Uzbekistan and its neighbors.[26] The dirty-war methods employed by certain Latin American states and apartheid South Africa during the 1970s and 1980s (incorporating death squads, "disappearances," and the extra-judicial killings of peaceful dissenters) also offer negative examples that democracies should avoid, not just because they are unethical, but because they also undermine the legal foundations upon which a government's legitimacy and credibility with its citizens are founded.[27]

There are limitations to the scope of this paper that the author acknowledges, most notably that it does not examine in any detail the troubled state of the U.S./NATO campaign in Afghanistan (in particular, the controversial circumstances behind General Stanley McChrystal's dismissal in June 2010). It is not the author's intention to write a guide on how to win in Afghanistan or how to win the Long War. It is important to emphasize here that the United States and other partners may prevail in a COIN campaign, without necessarily achieving a strategic success in counterterrorism. Likewise, states may achieve positive results in thwarting terrorist attacks in their own countries without addressing the sources of instability overseas — a prime example here being the series of terrorist plots thwarted by the British police and MI5 since 2006, and the impotence of the UK authorities in countering the training of British-Muslim militants in Pakistan. As Thomas Rid and Thomas Keaney observe, "succeeding against an insurgency and succeeding against specific terrorists that are part of a wider global ideological movement may be two different things." As noted in the conclusion, the debate over counterterrorism and COIN in Afghanistan rests on two completely different strategic calculations as to what Operation ENDURING FREEDOM is supposed to achieve.[28]

There is also a risk that current debates on terrorism will be focused almost exclusively with reference to al-Qaeda and affiliated groups. It would be foolish to rule out a resurgence of ethno-nationalist or politically extremist terror in future decades, which is why this manuscript examines historical cases with reference to groups such as the Provisional Irish Republican Army (PIRA), Euskadi Ta Askatasuna (Basque Homeland and Liberty in Spain [ETA]), Fatah (the Movement for the National Liberation of Palestine), and the Red Army Faction.[29] The key point here is that political and strategic calculations provide the context in which military means are employed in any form of conflict, and counterterrorism can either be incorporated as part of the armed forces, COIN, or stabilization doctrine, or in a domestic context within what the British armed forces refer to as Military Aid to the Civil Authority (MACA).[30]

Before discussing the use of armed forces in counterterrorism, it is necessary first to define what constitutes terrorism, and also to address the controversy surrounding how this phenomenon is to be addressed. This debate revolves around the difficult question of whether terrorism is a crime or an act of war, and whether its practitioners end their campaigns because they are defeated, contained, or mollified by state authorities. This manuscript will then discuss the counterterrorist framework, before critically examining the military contribution to counterterrorism as far as democracies are concerned. In this respect, a state's armed forces can be employed on an ad hoc basis (in situations where it has specific capabilities that the civil authorities require in the short term), or as part of a prolonged engagement. The author will describe the full range of actions that armed forces can perform in counterterrorism—not merely the more sensational ones, such as hostage rescue, but nonkinetic operations such as deterrence, military assistance to civil authorities, and intelligence-gathering—and will also summarize the possible problems that may arise both in the international and domestic sphere when such means are employed in the fight against terrorism.

The main conclusion of this paper is that there are specific scenarios and situations in which a military response to terrorism is essential, be it on a short-term or prolonged basis, but that military measures have to be firmly integrated within an overall, politically directed strategy to contain terrorism and remove the grievances that national and transnational terrorist groups exploit. Furthermore, democratic governments are obliged to consider the potentially negative consequences of employing military force prior to deciding whether to hand specific counterterrorist missions over to their generals and admirals. At the heart of this analysis is the dilemma facing all democratic states confronted by terrorism; namely, how they fight this threat and protect their citizens without undermining the constitutional, legal, and normative characteristics upon which government by consent is founded.[31] The author does not promise to offer easy answers to this dilemma, nor to the challenges arising from it, but it is his hope that his examination of this topic provokes the debate and reflection that can provide the basis for both an informed consensus, as well as discussions about workable solutions to a perennial problem.

IS TERRORISM A MILITARY PROBLEM?

For nonacademics, the outlining of definitions may appear pedantic. Yet it is important to define our terminology, as an individual's perception of any intellectual problem is shaped by his or her understanding of concepts that can otherwise be taken for granted (terrorism, democracy, the military, etc.). A specific viewpoint on the characteristics and causes of terrorism shapes perceptions about whether a state can employ its armed forces as part of its effort to contain and ultimately defeat terrorism, or whether the use of military means would be counterproductive.[32]

With few exceptions, states maintain their own armed forces, which are configured, trained, and organized to fight a state-based adversary, although they can also be employed on peacekeeping/peace-support missions, as is the case with some Western countries in stabilization/COIN missions overseas.[33] In the United States, the UK, and certain other Western countries, there is a clear distinction between the military and the constabulary services employed for domestic policing; the latter are civilian organizations, and are lightly armed or (in the case of the UK) largely unarmed when they exercise their everyday duties. However, other states may have internal security forces trained and equipped on paramilitary lines. While the French *gendarmerie* and the Italian *carabinieri* are recognizable as police units, the Turkish *jandarma*, the Russian Interior Ministry (MVD) troops (*vnutrenniye voiska*), and the Indian Border Security Force (BSF) and Rashtriya Rifles (RR) are militarized forces in terms of their organization and their armament, and all have participated in combat operations against, respectively, the Kurdistan Worker's Party (PKK), Chechen rebels, and Kashmiri insurgents.[34] In the U.S. case, the CIA not only has its own paramilitary arm (the Special Activities Division), but it also controls the unmanned, armed drones used in targeted killings of terrorist leaders.[35] It is also alleged that the Blackwater Private Military Company (or Xe Services, its current name) has covertly cooperated with U.S. Special Forces and the Pakistani authorities in both targeted killings and snatch operations against al-Qaeda suspects in Pakistan.[36] These distinctions are worth noting, as in certain cases a military response by a democratic or democratizing country may not involve the employment of a regular army, navy, or air force.

This paper uses Fareed Zakaria's definition of a liberal democracy as "a political system marked not only by free and fair elections, but also by the rule of law, a separation of powers, and the protection of basic liberties of speech, assembly, religion, and property."[37] Liberal democratic states differ from nonliberal ones (such as Russia), in which the formal characteristics of a democracy, such as regular elections for the executive and legislature, are observed, but where significant constraints exist on civil liberties and freedom of speech. Established liberal democracies also differ

14

in character from democratizing states undergoing a transition from totalitarian/authoritarian rule to representative government — a prime example here being Turkey's transition since the 1990s, and the gradual erosion of the military's dominance over national politics in that nation.[38] The distinction is worth noting, insofar as politicians and senior military and security force personnel conditioned to operate in a dictatorial system may resort to old regime methods when dealing with internal security threats. For example, the Russian state's response to Chechen separatism owes much to the repressive traditions of the Soviet and Tsarist regimes.[39]

As noted below, there is no internationally accepted definition of terrorism, although the author concurs with Magnus Ranstorp and Paul Wilkinson's reference to:

> [The] systematic use of coercive intimidation usually, though not exclusively, to service political ends. It is used to create and exploit a climate of fear among a wider group than the immediate victims of the violence, often to publicise a cause, as well as to coerce a target into acceding to terrorist aims. Terrorism may be used on its own, or as part of a wider conventional war. It can be employed by desperate and weak minorities, by states as a tool of domestic or foreign policy, or by belligerents as an accompaniment or additional weapon in all types and stages of warfare.[40]

Alex Schmid identifies four intrinsic factors, which affect a liberal democracy's response to nonstate terrorism: freedom of movement, freedom of association, abundance of targets, and the constraints of the legal system. Democratic norms also stress openness, tolerance, legality and the high value of each individual human life (hence the fact that very few liberal democracies have the death penalty).[41] This can affect a state's counterterrorist policy in a number of ways, as shown in the British case both by Labour's efforts to introduce identity cards (which the Conservative-Liberal Democrat coalition opted to abolish soon after it assumed office in May 2010), and also the legal effort to block the extradition of radical Islamist clerics to their home countries, where they might be arrested and tortured. They have historically manifested themselves in instances where domestic critics highlight human rights abuses committed by the military and security services in conflicts of decolonization (as was the case with the British in Cyprus and the French in Algeria from 1954-62), and also in current cases where Western powers have become involved in overseas military interventions within the context of the War on Terror.[42] The persistent articulation of these norms is a sign of a healthy democracy, but it also shows how intrinsically controversial it is for a state to become involved in the fight against terrorists, whether in the domestic or international sphere.

The Conceptual Framework.

For Western democracies, "terrorism" traditionally occurred in wars of decolonization, such as the National Liberation Front's (FLN) campaign against French rule in Algeria, or the series of conflicts involving the British—notably the Irish War of Independence (1918-22), the struggle against *Irgun* and *Lehi* in Palestine (1944-48), EOKA's campaign for *Enosis* (unification) between Greece and Cyprus, and the Aden insurgency (1964-67). The late-1960s and early-1970s led to a rise in domestic terrorism in Western Europe, whether ethno-nationalist (notably the PIRA and its

Loyalist foes in Northern Ireland and the ETA in the Basque region of Spain) or politically radical like the Red Army Faction in West Germany; [BR] in Italy, November 17 [N17] in Greece, and *Action Directe* in France).

The same period also saw the internationalization of terrorism by the Palestinian Liberation Organization (PLO) and rival groups such as the Popular Front for the Liberation of Palestine (PFLP), which was responsible for the multiple hijacking of passenger aircraft on September 7, 1970. While this brand of transnational terror had the specific goal of publicizing the Palestinian cause, the globalized effort of al-Qaeda and its affiliates from the mid-1990s has more ambitious goals: to expel Western influence from the Islamic world, and to eventually establish a global caliphate.[43]

At present, there is no internationally recognized definition of what constitutes terrorism. Some states, notably Arab countries, eschew definitions that criminalize the use of violence as a tool for national self-determination, while the belief within Western left-wing circles that terrorism can be a legitimate means of self-defense on the part of oppressed peoples derives from Frantz Fanon's *Les Damnes de la Terre* (1962).[44] In this vein, commentators such as Noam Chomsky are quick to accuse the United States and certain other countries (such as the UK and Israel) of being terrorist states due to their employment of military force against weaker countries, while ignoring (or even excusing) cases on nonstate terrorism or examples of state terror which cannot be blamed on the West.[45] There are more nuanced and less strident versions of this argument, which may deplore the characteristics of terrorism while recognizing that its practitioners may have justifiable motives. Terrorism is described as a strategy of the weak (Lawrence Freedman[46]) and as the poor man's air force; these statements should not be seen as implying moral equivalence between state and nonstate groups, but merely recognition that some of the latter, and their state sponsors, use terrorism as a cheap and easy way of retaliating against a stronger adversary.[47] A prime example of this process occurred when Colonel Muammar Gaddafi increased arms supplies to the PIRA after the British government gave its U.S. ally permission to use airbases in the UK to support air strikes on Libya in April 1986.[48]

To a certain degree, the plight of a particular ethnic or national group can be treated as a factor behind terrorist violence. It is possible to condemn suicide attacks against Israeli civilians, but also recognize that the dispossession of the Palestinian people in 1948 and their lack of statehood are contributory causes of Palestinian terrorism. Nevertheless, gross injustice does not necessarily force its victims to adopt terrorism as a means of resistance. From the late 1970s to July 1989, *Solidarnosc* (Solidarity) waged a campaign of civil disobedience against the Polish Communist regime, eschewing violence even when the authorities used force against their own citizenry; as was the case after the declaration of martial law by General Wojciech Jaruzelski in December 1981. This decision on the part of Polish dissidents was influenced to a considerable degree by ethical considerations and a desire to retain the moral high ground (a calculation reinforced by their ties to the Catholic Church), although *Solidarnosc* activists were also aware that a general insurrection could provoke a Soviet military intervention.[49]

The words "terrorist" and "terrorism" are pejorative, as they automatically imply amorality and barbaric ruthlessness on the part of their practitioners. This explains why Western media agencies such as the BBC employ less value-laden language in their news reports, employing phrases such as "militants," "separatists," "guerillas," and "insurgents." For the victims of terrorism, this approach can be seen as deceitful equivocation.[50] Although the author of this manuscript offers his own definitions of what a terrorist is, he too uses other phrases to describe them ("gunmen," "hostage takers," etc.), for no underlying reason other than to avoid repetition.

For the purposes of this paper, the author will focus on examples where armed nonstate groups have employed lethal violence in order to intimidate their target(s) — one government or several, or a particular national community — into acceding to their political demands. Terrorism can be a domestic or an international phenomenon, and its practitioners can launch attacks within a specific country that are not actually directed against that particular government or its people. PIRA attacks in Germany and Holland in 1988-89 were directed against British military personnel stationed in both countries, while the six ethnic Arab (Ahvaz) gunmen who took over the Iranian embassy in London on April 30, 1980, had no grievance with the UK, as opposed to the theocratic regime in Tehran.[51] Nonetheless, the consequences of terrorist violence are often felt by innocent third parties; Al-Qaeda's targets in the Nairobi and Dar-es-Salaam bombings of August 7, 1998, were the U.S. embassies in both cities, but the majority of those killed and maimed by both attacks were Kenyan and Tanzanian bystanders.[52]

Bruce Hoffman draws a distinction between old terrorist groups that had relatively limited objectives, and were comparatively more scrupulous about minimizing casualties caused by their attacks, and new terrorists who possess global ambitions and often have eschatological or anti-systemic objectives.[53] The latter no longer conform to Brian Jenkins's statement about terrorists launching attacks that leave "a lot of people watching, and a lot of people listening, and not a lot of people dead."[54] There is also a contrast to be drawn between the defined hierarchical structure of traditional groups (notably that of PIRA, with its Army Council, chief of staff, general headquarters [GHQ], and other military trappings), and what John Arquilla and David Ronfeldt refer to as "netwar," in which "dispersed organizations, small groups and individuals ... communicate, coordinate and conduct their campaign in an internetted manner, without a precise central command."[55] In this respect, in the aftermath of 9/11, al-Qaeda provides an example of franchise terrorism in which the Internet is used to share information on tactics and technology (notably on bomb construction), and in which the leadership inspires but does not direct sympathizers across the globe to conduct acts of violence against their host societies.[56] The implications for this trend for any counterterrorist strategy are disturbing, as a protean network is far less easy for a state's security forces to attack and weaken by attrition than a centrally-commanded group organized along quasi-military lines.[57]

Terrorism can also be incorporated as part of a wider campaign of insurgency, defined as a paramilitary and subversive effort waged by an irregular armed faction, or factions, to overthrow a state's government, to secede from a state, or (in the case of Hamas regarding Israel) to destroy the state.[58] The example set by the Karen and other rebel groups in Burma shows that it is possible for insurgents to eschew terrorism. The Patani United Liberation Organisation currently waging an insurgency in Southern Thailand has also declared that it will not conduct bombings beyond its Muslim heartland, recognizing that attacks in Bangkok or in tourist resorts will attract hostile international attention. It is also true that some terrorist organizations lack the means to threaten their adversaries with a wider insurgency (as was the case with European terrorist groups such as the ETA and the Red Army Faction, and also PIRA after the early 1970s).[59] Yet, in other cases, terrorism can be merged within a wider insurgent threat to state stability or state survival, as with the Revolutionary Armed Forces in Colombia (FARC) and the Sunni Arab *muqawamah* (resistance) fighting the Coalition and the post-Baathist government in Iraq. Prior to its defeat in May 2009, the Liberation Tigers of Tamil Eelam (LTTE) posed such a significant military threat to the Sri Lankan government, which included its own small navy and air force, that the latter had to use its armed forces to crush it.[60] The same can be said of the *Tehrik e-Taleban Pakistan* (TTP), an alliance of militant Pashtun tribesmen and foreign fighters that has not only waged an insurgency in the FATA since 2004, but has also been responsible for supporting a series of terrorist attacks in Pakistan conducted by allied jihadi groups (including, Islamabad alleges, the suicide bombing that killed former President Benazir Bhutto in December 2007).[61] If a terrorist group has the numbers, resources, and sufficient popular support to threaten the government's authority, then a state's counterterrorist policy has to be incorporated within a wider COIN strategy.

COIN involves the coordinated response of a state's government and its external supporters to integrate political, socioeconomic, legal, police, and military measures to frustrate and ultimately defeat an insurgency. Within that framework, counterterrorism includes defensive measures to minimize the ability of a terrorist/insurgent group to inflict violence against the civilian population; examples here include emergency legislation to ban membership in an organization and its political wing, increased police and military patrols in public places, and information campaigns to inspire public vigilance against potential attacks. An enlightened counterterrorism policy will also attempt to strike a balance between public safety and civil liberties, and will acknowledge the need for policies that alleviate the causes of terrorism. This will involve measures to alleviate popular grievances that terrorist groups exploit, and promote dialogue with community leaders and political figures who may be sympathetic to the terrorists' cause, if not their methods.[62] Counterterrorism does, however, incorporate more offensive measures to undermine terrorist groups and neutralize its members. These include the recruitment of terrorists to inform on their comrades (to work as agents), and also the turning of captured members of a group (preferably through persuasion, not coercion) so that they provide intelligence on their former comrades.[63]

Democratic norms dictate that neutralization should ideally involve arrest, followed by the established procedures of trial by due process, conviction, and incarceration. Yet neutralization can also involve the killing of terrorists by members of the security forces. This can either be because the former are armed and resist arrest, or because they are in the process of committing a violent act, in which case soldiers or police act under rules of engagement (ROE) permitting self-defense. The British Army in Northern Ireland

22

was theoretically bound by the Yellow Card each soldier carried, which authorized the use of deadly force solely in circumstances in which soldiers felt that their lives were at risk; for example, in a situation when a suspect appeared likely to use a firearm or explosive device against them. However, in Northern Ireland, as in other cases, critics allege that lethal violence is used because there is a specific, if undeclared, policy to kill suspected terrorists rather than capture them. As noted below, some states, notably Israel, have conducted targeted killings, and the French example in Algeria shows that in a permissive environment even a democratic state's military and security forces can employ unpalatable measures such as torture and extrajudicial executions against suspected terrorists.[64]

The British government's current, declared counterterrorist policy acknowledges the multifaceted nature of the terrorist threat, and the means needed to address it. The Ministry of Defense's (MOD) *Strategic Defence Review: A New Chapter* (2002) and *Delivering Security in a Changing World* (2003) both committed the UK armed forces to a more overt role in counterterrorism, both in intervention operations overseas (notably Afghanistan) but also in domestic security.[65] However, the main document expressing British government policy in dealing with the post-9/11 terrorist threat is the Counter-Terrorism Strategy (CONTEST) paper first published in 2006, and then revised 3 years later. The declared aim of British counterterrorism policy is: "to reduce the risk to the UK and its interests overseas from international terrorism, so that people can go about their lives freely and with confidence.[66]

According to CONTEST, the UK's approach to counterterrorism involves (1) the **prevention** of terrorism by tackling its causes, (2) the **pursuit** of terrorists and their sponsors, (3) the **protection** of the public and key services, and (4) **preparation** to respond to and mitigate the consequences of a terrorist attack. CONTEST places the Home Office as the lead agency for domestic counterterrorism, and the Foreign and Commonwealth Office (FCO) as the key Ministry overseeing its international aspects, while the MOD supports both departments. CONTEST emphasizes the primacy of political and nonmilitary means of fighting terrorism. These include the need to isolate the terrorist physically and psychologically from the wider population, and to use other levers of national power (notably the diplomatic and economic) to resolve the grievances that cause terrorism (such as the radicalization of young British Muslims).[67] Nonetheless, CONTEST also has an explicit military dimension. The UK's armed forces are explicitly committed to **prevention** and **pursuit** (most notably in the context of current operations in Afghanistan). Specialist elements are committed to **protection** (notably the interceptors of the Royal Air Force's Quick Reaction Alert [QRA] force) and, at least nominally, to **preparation**, this being the declared role of the Civil Contingency Reaction Force (CCRF) announced in the 2002 *New Chapter*, which is supposedly drawn from the British armed forces reserve units.

Criminality or Warfare?

Scholars of terrorism identify two distinct models that a state can employ in response to this threat. The criminal justice approach treats terrorism as a law-and-order issue, and although the government may introduce emergency legislation to bolster the state's legal framework, it is the judiciary and the police that play the lead role in implementing counterterrorist measures. The war model, in contrast, treats terrorism as a mortal threat to the state, which can only be addressed by military force.[68] The latter is more or less the default approach of an illiberal state such as post-Communist Russia. After a series of bombings in Russian cities during September 1999, which were blamed on Chechen separatists, President Putin declared the latter would be "wasted in the shit-house," and that his government and its security forces would "quickly, decisively, with clenched teeth, strangle the vermin at the root." In a similar vein, the Russian President responded to the Beslan massacre of September 2004 with the pledge to "wipe out all terrorist scum, no matter where they are." Such rhetoric reflected the prevailing state of public opinion within Russian society.[69]

As Audrey Kurth Cronin observes, terrorism picks "at the vulnerable seam between domestic law and foreign war . . . [arguing] over which paradigm best fits the threat — war or crime — says more about the rigid intellectual and bureaucratic structures of the state than it does about the nature of terrorism."[70] It is therefore unsurprising that in practice many democracies adopt counterterrorist policies that contain elements of both models, and the degree to which an individual country conforms closest to the criminal justice or war model depends on the following factors:

Constitutional framework and normative constraints. Prior to 9/11, the U.S. military operated under the constraints of the *Posse Comitatus Act* (1876), which imposed restrictions on the use of the armed forces in domestic policing.[71] In contrast, Britain has a tradition of using its armed forces as part of a policy of Military Aid to the Civil Authority (MACA), discussed in more detail later. Aside from the small size of the Red Army Faction and affiliated groups, one of the principal reasons why the Federal Republic of Germany (FRG) made the police the lead agency in the fight against far-left terrorism was that its political elite was determined to avoid the excesses of the Nazi era, and to ensure that the balance between civil liberties and security favored the former. The Greek government's reluctance to crack down on N17 until the late 1990s derived in part from political and popular disgust with the repressive record of the military *junta* between 1967 and 1974.[72]

How lethal are they? The main indicator of the threat that a terrorist group—or groups—poses to a particular state is proportionate to the numbers within the organization and its ability to mount serial and deadly attacks against civil society. The lowest-level example is that of so-called lone wolves like David Copeland, the British neo-Nazi responsible for three bomb attacks in London in the spring of 1999. Leftist terrorists in West Germany never managed recruitment beyond double figures (25-32 at most), and between 1969-79 managed just 63 attacks (bombings, bank raids, kidnappings, and assassinations), which claimed 33 lives. There was therefore little public or political pressure to call in the *Bundeswehr* to deal with them.[73]

The BR was, however, a larger and deadlier group, being responsible for increasing terrorist violence in Italy during the late 1970s: 467 attacks in 1975; 685 in 1976; 1,806 in 1977; and 2,275 in 1978. Given the extent of this activity, and the public alarm aroused by the kidnapping of former Prime Minister Aldo Moro on March 16, 1978, and his murder 54 days later, it is surprising that the Italian state persisted with a police-centric campaign against the BR, let alone an adherence to the rule of law. The normative constraints noted above (in this case, institutional and public memories of Fascism) clearly shaped the Italian response; hence, the quote attributed to *carabinieri* General Carlo Dalla Chiesa when a subordinate suggested that BR suspects could be interrogated more harshly to help the security forces find Moro, "Italy can survive the loss of Aldo Moro. It would not survive the introduction of torture."[74]

A contrasting example can be seen with Israel's reaction to Palestinian attacks from the Munich massacre of 1972 and Ma'alot atrocity of May 15, 1974 — in which the Democratic Front for the Liberation of Palestine (DFLP) massacred 22 schoolchildren — to the first Hamas suicide bombing in Israel on April 16, 1994. Between 1994 and 2007, suicide attacks have killed several hundred Israelis. Reprisals have included the targeted killings of militant leaders and key figures and retaliatory attacks against targets in both the occupied territories and neighboring countries.[75] On the extreme end of the lethality scale, albeit in a nondemocratic state, one can see the example of the Armed Islamic Group (GIA) and the Group for Preaching and Combat (GSPC) insurgents in Algeria during the civil war of 1992-2002. Islamist terrorists from both groups were involved in a series of barbaric atrocities (including the extermination of entire villages) in a conflict that killed up to 100,000 people. Although the Algerian state's own extensive human rights abuses cannot be condoned, it is important to note that the scale of GIA and GSPC violence obliged it to adopt a militarized response.[76]

Are they a domestic or international phenomenon? A terrorist group operating in one democratic state may be contained by the existing legal-police framework, particularly if it lacks widespread popular support. However, if it operates on a regional or global level, these means may be insufficient, particularly if the terrorists can rely on an overseas sanctuary. For example, in the United States, domestic terrorists from the Weathermen during the 1970s to the Unabomber and far-right militia groups of the 1990s could be contained by the Federal Bureau of Investigation (FBI). The same could not be said of al-Qaeda, with its global presence and more wide-ranging scale of activity and support.[77]

State sponsorship. State support can have a dramatic impact on the effectiveness and lethality of a terrorist organization. Sympathetic governments can provide sanctuary, funding, training (including specialist knowledge in more sophisticated techniques, such as bomb construction and commando-type tactics, from intelligence and military personnel), and arms (from assault rifles to surface-to-air missiles). Poorly armed and incompetent terrorists can be beaten by an ordinary constabulary and its criminal investigative/ Special Branch elements; they are also more liable to suffer from their own efforts, for example, being blown up by their own bombs while assembling or planting them. Yet state support can effect a quantitative improvement in the operational effectiveness of a terrorist group. A prime example is that of the Red Army Faction after the East German secret police, the *Ministerium fur Staatssicherheit*, provided the Faction with sanctuary and training in the former German Democratic Republic (GDR). The Red Army staged fewer attacks than before receiving East German support, but these were far more professionally executed than they had been previously—one example being the bombing that nearly killed the Supreme Allied Commander of NATO Forces in Europe, General Alexander Haig, on June 25, 1979. Likewise, PIRA's capabilities were significantly enhanced when it received Libyan arms (including heavy weaponry and Semtex plastic explosive) from the mid-1980s, although as noted in the next chapter the loss of the bulk of these weapons with the interception of the *Eksund* (October 1987) was a serious blow to this organization.[78]

State support can provide terrorist groups with significant military capabilities. The PLO (notably Yasser Arafat's Fatah) and its rivals formed substantial private armies in Jordan (before September 1970) and Lebanon, thanks to lavish assistance from the Soviet bloc, Egypt, Syria, Libya, Algeria, Iraq, and subsequently Iran. Hezbollah's evolution into a sophisticated guerrilla/terrorist force depended principally on training from *Sepah e-Pasdaran* (Iranian Revolutionary Guard Corps) cadres based in the Bekaa Valley during the 1980s.[79]

Are they a wider threat to state stability? Certain terrorist groups have a purely parasitic relationship with society, having no significant supporting constituency — a prime example in this regard being the German Red Army Faction. However, in other cases, such as PIRA and ETA, these organizations can rely on a support base within civil society. If a terrorist campaign is waged concurrently with widespread civil disorder and strife (for example, in Northern Ireland in the early 1970s, or Kashmir from 1989) or it exists alongside an existential threat to the state — as posed by many of Israel's neighbors historically, and Iran currently — then it is more likely that a government might resort to the military means outlined below. Israel has adopted a deterrence-based response to the PLO and, currently,

Hamas and Hezbollah, as its political and military leadership fear that an irresolute response will convey weakness, inspiring further offensive action that may lead to an all-out attack on the Jewish state by its internal and external enemies.[80]

As far as MACA is concerned, the British Army was originally deployed in Northern Ireland in August 1969 because the Royal Ulster Constabulary (RUC) was unable to contain widespread rioting by Catholics and intersectarian conflict between the latter and the Protestants. In fact the RUC (and its B Special reservists) was very much part of the problem because of its pro-Protestant partisanship and heavy-handed treatment of the Catholic community — as shown by the excessive violence police had employed against peaceful civil rights demonstrations in October 1968. A combination of ham-fisted British policy and PIRA militancy led to a low-level insurgency during the early 1970s, but once the British Army began to contain terrorist violence, the British government moved toward a policy of police primacy, designating a reformed RUC (from 1976) as the lead agency over the military in the struggle against terrorism. Although a substantial military presence was required in Northern Ireland until after the Good Friday Accords, the British authorities were determined that the local police should play a more prominent role in providing security once both the threat of insurgency and civil war between Catholics and Protestants had been quelled.[81]

So are terrorists soldiers or criminals? Most terrorist groups, save those capable of waging an insurgency concurrently, lack the military capabilities needed to engage a state's armed forces on the latter's terms. Yet they still employ military nomenclature when describing their organizations and their objectives, and it is rare for any organization to accept the terrorist label.[82] This is evident from the Irish Republican volunteers serving in Brigades and Companies, and also in the martyrdom video of the ringleader of the four suicide bombers involved in the July 7, 2005, attacks on London; Mohammed Siddique Khan justified his actions and those of his associates by stating that "[we] are at war, and I am a soldier."[83] This militarized ethos is also illustrated by bin Laden's declaration of war against the Jews and Crusaders (February 23, 1998), and in the rhetoric that his subordinates used to justify 9/11. The attacks on New York and Washington, DC, were lauded by al-Qaeda propaganda as a means of mobilizing wider Muslim opinion against an America simultaneously condemned for being a global oppressor, and derided for being internally weak and decadent. Furthermore, as Daniel Benjamin and Steven Simon note, on 9/11, al-Qaeda conducted an attack on the United States which was warlike in its dimensions, in terms of the devastation caused and the losses (human, material, and financial) suffered. Critics of War on Terror rhetoric overlook the fact that the militarization of this current struggle is not a one-sided affair.[84]

If one accepts Clausewitz's statement that "war is an act of violence to compel our enemy to do our will," it is clear that acts of terrorism are not purely criminal in nature. Terrorist groups are, after all, seeking to use force to coerce their target(s) into acceding to their demands, whether these are for a united Ireland, a Tamil homeland, or the expulsion of Western influence from the Muslim world.[85] British General Frank Kitson stated that, "there can be no such thing as a purely military solution [in COIN] because insurgency is not primarily a military activity," there is also "no such thing as a wholly political solution . . . short of surrender, because the very fact that a state of insurgency exists implies that violence is involved which will have to be countered to some extent at least by the use of lethal force." [86] The same can be said of counterterrorism. While it is understandable that some analysts of terrorism do not wish to legitimize this phenomenon by ascribing to it the characteristics of state-based warfare, the essentially military character of terrorism should be acknowledged in addition to the fact that if a terrorist organization poses a significant threat to the security of a state, then the latter's armed forces — as deliverers of security to the society they serve — are likely to be involved in countering that threat.

It is commonly agreed by Western academics and informed commentators that a purely militaristic focus on counterterrorism is misconceived, but there are equally simplistic assumptions that need to be dispelled. The first is the fatuous statement that "one man's terrorist is another man's freedom fighter." This cliché can be dispelled by a straightforward comparison between (for example) Nelson Mandela and Andreas Baader. For Mandela, terrorism was a last resort. For Baader, it was an end in itself. Mandela expressed coherent and understandable reasons why the African National Congress' military wing, *Mkhonto we Sizwe*, took up arms, namely in order to liberate and enfranchise a politically oppressed and socioeconomically disadvantaged majority, and to overthrow a despotic and racist regime. Baader provided no clear rationale for the Red Army Faction's activities, other than expressing a vague notion of liberating a German proletariat with whom he and his comrades had nothing in common. Even within terrorist groups, one can see a vast difference in character, motivation, and technique between its members. PIRA, for example, could attract individuals like Francis Hughes—recognized by British Army officers as a committed professional, and one of the seven Provisional prisoners who starved themselves to death in the 1981 hunger strike. Yet the movement Hughes sacrificed himself for also attracted the mafia-type characters Eamon Collins condemned in his memoirs as a PIRA volunteer, not to mention the thugs who beat Robert McCartney to death in a Belfast pub on January 31, 2005.[87]

From the freedom fighter cliché comes another pernicious analogy: the idea that the default response to a terrorist campaign should be the pursuit of negotiations. Thomas Mockaitis draws a useful distinction between insurgents who have a viable cause (and who are ready to seek a compromise settlement with their foes) and terrorists whose "goals are so idealistic as to be virtually unattainable."[88] In contrast, former Northern Ireland Secretary Mo Mowlam and Jonathan Powell (one of Blair's former advisors) have argued that the Good Friday Accords offer a template for negotiations with al-Qaeda. Powell and Mowlam presumed that PIRA's goals and those of bin Laden were somehow comparable, and that it is as easy to achieve a nonviolent solution with those focussed on an apocalyptic struggle between Islam and a degenerate West as it is with a movement committed to a united Ireland.[89] It is also important to distinguish between terrorists whose objectives involve rectifying a gross injustice, and those who simply seek revenge. For example, the African National Congress (ANC) did not want a racial war against Afrikaaners; it sought a truly democratic South Africa in which both whites and blacks had equal rights before the state and the law.

The ANC was, after all, a multiracial organization, with white members such as Joe Slovo and Ronnie Kasrils. Hamas, by contrast, is an avowedly anti-Semitic organization, whose founding charter proclaims the inevitability of a final struggle in which "Muslims will fight the Jews" and destroy them. If Hamas ever achieved its objectives, the result would be the ethnic cleansing of Jews from Palestine. The argument that Israel is somehow duty bound to talk to enemies who seek its destruction is therefore an unrealistic one, and critics of Israel's military actions against Hamas should examine whether the latter's own ideological intransigence is in itself one of the sources of the current impasse in the Israeli-Palestinian peace process.[90]

In considering the potential for negotiation and reconciliation, it is also instructive to bear in mind the contrasting examples of two Islamists who turned to terrorism. The first is Imad Mugniyah, a senior Hezbollah military commander killed in a car bomb attack in Damascus on February 12, 2008 (attributed to, but not admitted by, *Mossad*). Mugniyah was described by U.S. and Israeli intelligence sources as the founder of Hezbollah's armed wing, the Islamic Resistance (IR), and the main instigator of attacks on Western targets in Lebanon during the 1980s. Mugniyah was also instrumental in conducting the IR's guerrilla campaign against the Israeli Defence Force (IDF) in Southern Lebanon until the latter's withdrawal in 2000.[91] David Barkai, a former IDF intelligence officer, described Mugniyah as follows:

> His is one of the most creative and brilliant minds I have ever come across. He is a man with deep understanding, an excellent technical grasp, and leadership ability. Unfortunately, a mixture of personal and geopolitical circumstances led him to channel his out-

standing talents into the path of blood and destruction and to make him into a dangerous enemy.[92]

Mugniyah was clearly a skilled practitioner of terrorism and guerrilla warfare, but showed no sign of having any overarching political perceptions, or any sign of compromising with his violent objectives toward the West or Israel. A contrast can be seen with Nasir Abbas, an Indonesian who became a member of *Jemaah Islamiyah*, al-Qaeda's Southeast Asian network. Abbas became a jihadi while fighting the Soviets in Afghanistan during the 1980s and believed that it was a good Muslim's duty to fight infidels occupying Islamic land. However, the Bali bombings on October 12, 2002, which killed 202 civilians, led him to become a police informant. Abbas saw the mass murder of nightclub revellers as a violation of what was supposed to be a defensive jihad against godless aggressors.[93] Some terrorists' motivations may compel them toward violence regardless of the cost, others may reassess and abandon their commitment to a lost or discredited cause. Western governments therefore have more prospects of negotiating and compromising with the Abbas's of this world than they would have with the Mugniyahs.

The "negotiations work" school also misses two further aspects of terrorism. The first is that groups with originally "just" goals may fight on even when these objectives have been achieved. The majority of Spanish Basques are satisfied with the autonomy that they were given after the demise of Franco and his regime in 1975 and do not support ETA's continued resort to violence. The second is that negotiations with an undefeated terrorist/insurgent organization can simply lead to the flouting of peace accords, as demonstrated by the failure of Colombian President Andres Pastrana's efforts to seek a settlement with FARC in the late 1990s.[94] A further example is offered by the Pakistani Army's repeated efforts to negotiate truces with the TTP in the FATA (in 2004, 2006, and 2008), which simply encouraged the latter to launch wider attacks to take over neighboring districts in the North-West Frontier Province (NWFP) in February 2009. The Army's decision to fight back and its recapture of Buner and Swat in July 2009 were applauded at that time by the majority of Pakistanis, who believed that peace agreements with the TTP inspired the latter toward further violence.[95]

Above all, claims that conflict resolution in Northern Ireland offers a model overlook the underlying reasons behind the Good Friday Accords. For all *Sinn Fein*'s propaganda, it is evident that by 1997 PIRA was militarily contained and frustrated by the British Army and the RUC, leaving the majority of Irish Republicans convinced that they had no option but to follow nonviolent political methods in pursuing their goals.[96] In certain cases, military and police operations can be integrated as part of an overall policy of containing and, if necessary, neutralizing hard-core terrorists who wish to fight to the bitter end, while impressing those amenable to compromise that negotiations offer a more viable means of achieving objectives than the continuation of violence.

To summarize, terrorism represents a strategic choice, namely a decision by an armed nonstate faction to use violence for political ends. Terrorists can be skilled guerrilla fighters or rank amateurs. They can be rational individuals who relate violence to the attainment of their political objectives, or sadistic thugs who revel in butchery for its own sake. They can be motivated by high-minded ideals or unmitigated malice toward their enemies/victims. They can adhere to coherent goals providing the basis for a diplomatic resolution, or aspire to boundlessly utopian or nihilistic ideas. Furthermore, all these types of terrorists can conceivably exist within one particular group or network. The assumption that the causes of terrorism can automatically be resolved by ushering its practitioners to the conference table is therefore as flawed as the belief that the latter can only be dealt with by force. In accepting that there may be conditions in which military power can be employed against terrorism, it is therefore easier to examine the specific tasks that a state's armed forces can perform in a counterterrorism campaign, which are outlined in the next section.

THE MILITARY'S ROLE IN COUNTERTERRORISM

Some of the tasks discussed here can be carried out by specialized police units. For example, the FRG's first dedicated counterterrorist unit (GSG9) was recruited in April 1973 not from the *Bundeswehr*, but from the border guards. In the same year, the French authorities raised the National Gendermerie Intervention Group (GIGN) from the ranks of the *gendarmerie*. Both of these formations have successfully stormed hijacked aircraft and rescued hostages—GSG9 in Mogadishu in October 1977 following the takeover of Lufthansa Flight 181 by the PFLP, and GIGN in Marseilles in December 1994 to recover Air France Flight 8969, taken over by the GIA in Algiers. Civil police forces usually have bomb disposal teams, and may also have a Chemical, Biological, Radiological and Nuclear (CBRN) response capability, such as that of the Metropolitan Police's Tactical Support Group, which can respond to a CBRN emergency in London.[97] However, there are contingencies that are beyond the capabilities or the training of a police service, and these can be summarized as follows:

Military Aid to the Civil Authority.

In British law, MACA is defined as the employment of the UK's armed forces by the government in circumstances beyond traditional disturbances to the peace. MACA can be subdivided into Military Aid to the Civil Power (MACP), which involves the use of the armed forces to assist the civil authorities in the restoration of law and order, and Military Aid to the Civil Community (MACC), usually involving disaster relief, but also including specific responses to a mass casualty terrorist attack. Western armed forces have specialized units such as the UK's Joint CBRN Regiment, a British Army-Royal Air Force (RAF) formation, trained in the containment and decontamination processes needed in the aftermath of a major CBRN attack. This theoretical capability was available from the Japanese Self-Defence Force during the Sarin gas attack committed by *Aum Shinrikyo* on the Tokyo subway system on March 20, 1995, although this incident was on such a small scale that the police and emergency services were able to contain and decontaminate the stations affected and also treat most casualties successfully.[98]

A further contingency within MACC involves the scrambling of fighter jets to shoot down a hijacked airliner in order to prevent a 9/11-style atrocity. In Britain's case, the responsibility for responding to such a scenario is allocated to the QRA force based at RAF

Coningsby. In all of these contingencies, there has to be a clear request from the Home Office to the MOD, and the decision to deploy military units on MACA tasks requires ministerial approval. The criteria that need to be met are: The use of the armed forces has to be an action of last resort; lives must be judged to be in danger if military assistance is not requested; and the military can only use resources under their own direct command and can only follow a clear request for assistance from civilian police chiefs endorsed by ministerial approval.[99] The practical application of MACA can be seen in May 1980, during the Iranian Embassy siege. After the hostage takers murdered an Iranian diplomat, the Metropolitan Police relayed a request for military intervention through the emergency committee meeting in the Cabinet Office Briefing Room A (COBRA). COBRA was established in the aftermath of the Munich Olympics massacre in 1972, and its bureaucratic framework for crisis management still operates according to that initiated with the Iranian Embassy siege 30 years ago.[100]

The best-known example of MACP in a democratic state is that of Operation BANNER, the deployment of the UK armed forces (principally the British Army) to Northern Ireland from 1969-2007. As noted earlier, the problem of terrorist violence was compounded by a low-level sectarian civil war, while the lead civil policing agency was associated by the Catholic community with the discriminatory and oppressive policies of the Protestant/Unionist hierarchy, which dominated the devolved Parliament in Stormont.[101] A lesser-known example was the deployment of Canadian troops under the War Powers Act in Quebec during October 1970 at the request of the provincial Premier and the Mayor of Montreal. In this case, the Canadian Forces acted in a supporting role, leaving the task of arresting and detaining members of the separatist *Front de Liberation du Quebec* (FLQ) to the local police.[102]

Deterrence.

The military can also be deployed in a preventative role if the authorities receive intelligence indicating that a terrorist attack is imminent. Any public venue where large numbers of people congregate, such as a major sporting event or an airport, offers a natural target for an atrocity (for example, the attack by the Japanese Red Army on Lod Airport in May 1972; the Munich Olympics Massacre in September 1972; attacks on passengers by the Abu Nidal Organisation [ANO] at the Rome and Vienna airports in December 1985; and the failed attack on Glasgow airport in July 2007 by Islamist militants). Examples of deterrence operations include the deployment of troops to Heathrow airport on January 5-6, 1974, in response to an apparent plot by Palestinian terrorists to shoot down airliners with portable anti-aircraft missiles.[103] As a result of the Lod and Munich atrocities, the British MOD drafted contingency plans to preempt an attack at Heathrow (known as Operation MARMION), and these plans were implemented in January 1974, with 150 soldiers and 180 extra police deployed to patrol London's principal air terminal. In February 2003, there was a similar operation at the same airport, initiated by the Blair government in response to intelligence indicating an imminent al-Qaeda attack.[104]

Interdiction.

Maritime and air forces can be employed in the interception of terrorist personnel and arms shipments. The IDF has two significant successes to its credit. The first was the seizure of the *Karine-A* by the Israeli Navy on January 3, 2002. The vessel was carrying $15 million worth of weapons from Iran to the Palestinian Authority, which the Israelis presumed would be employed in the *intifada* in the occupied territories. The second was the capture of the *Francop* by the Israeli Navy's Special Forces (*Shayetet* 13) on November 4, 2009. This vessel is reported to have been carrying rockets, mortar shells, grenades, and small arms ammunition from Iran, apparently for Hezbollah.[105]

The Royal Navy was involved in maritime interdiction patrols during the troubles in Northern Ireland, assisted by the Irish Naval Service (INS) as well as the French authorities. The INS captured two trawlers carrying arms for PIRA—the *Claudia* on March 28, 1973, (with a Libyan weapons shipment) and the *Marita Ann* on September 24, 1984, (which had arms purchased from the United States on board) with the Royal Navy and RAF providing surveillance support. French customs officers intercepted the *Eksund* in October 1987 (a merchant vessel carrying 150 tons of Libyan weaponry), but it is reported that during its voyage from Tripoli the *Eksund* was under observation from unidentified military aircraft, and its cargo was also betrayed to the British and Irish intelligence services by a mole within PIRA. Although prior to the autumn of 1987 PIRA had managed to smuggle in smaller quantities of Libyan arms, the lost of the *Eksund* and its cargo was a major disaster for this group. It thwarted PIRA's plans to escalate its operations with heavier weaponry, and to launch a Tet-like offensive, which would inflict significant losses on the British armed forces and the RUC, undermining Britain's will to continue the anti-terrorist struggle in Northern Ireland. Furthermore, the Libyans blamed the *Eksund*'s loss on inadequate security measures, cutting off aid to Irish Republican terrorists as a consequence.[106]

More current examples include the involvement of NATO and other navies in Operation ACTIVE ENDEAVOUR since October 4, 2001. This involves a combination of deterrence and interdiction, patrolling choke points such as the Straits of Gibraltar and also boarding vessels suspected of carrying illicit passengers or cargo. The U.S.-led Combined Task Force 150 (CTF150) off the Horn of Africa provides another example, although its activity has since been subsumed into anti-piracy operations off the coast of Somalia and Yemen.[107] The efficacy of these operations can be questioned. For example, U.S. and allied naval patrols in the Arabian Sea/Persian Gulf region have been intensive (Coalition forces boarded 180 ships in the 10 months following 9/11), but have detained no al-Qaeda terrorists. The scale of arms trafficking in sensitive regions, notably the Red Sea/Gulf of Aden zone, also suggests that naval missions such as CTF150 are overstretched, particularly if they are also expected to quell Somali pirates.[108] Furthermore, maritime operations like ACTIVE ENDEAVOUR do little to stop non-state groups from acquiring weapons within Europe, whether from organized criminal groups such as the Neapolitan Camorra, or free-lance dealers such as the Russian arms trafficker Viktor Bout.[109]

Two examples of air interdiction suggest that such a process works best on the basis of precise intelligence. The first involves the interception by U.S. Navy fighters of an Egyptian airliner carrying the Palestine Liberation Front (PLF) hijackers of the *Achille Lauro* on October 10, 1985. The plane was forced to land at Sigonella Naval Air Station in Sicily, where, after a tense stand-off between U.S. Special Forces and the *carabinieri*, the PLF terrorists were handed over to Italian custody. A more recent occurrence was the air-strike conducted on an arms convoy of around 23 trucks crossing Sudan in March 2009. The convoy, which was destroyed either by the Israeli air force or UAVs, is supposed to have carried Iranian arms for Hamas.[110]

Training Allied Forces.

Since September 2001, Western armed forces have become increasingly involved in providing counterterrorist training to the military and security forces of friendly governments in regions where Islamist extremists are active. This includes U.S. assistance to Central Asian military forces, notably those of Uzbekistan and Kyrgyzstan,[111] and also the American-led Combined Joint Task Force-Horn of Africa (CJTF-HOA), located at Camp Lemonier in Djibouti, which trains allied African military personnel. Camp Lemonier also allegedly provides a base for U.S. Special Forces operations throughout the Horn of Africa and Yemen. Since October 2008, CJTF-HOA has been under the command of the U.S. military's Africa Command (AFRICOM), established in response to Washington's concerns over ungoverned spaces on the continent and their potential for developing as havens for al-Qaeda and other transnational terrorist groups. As of 2010, AFRICOM has a staff of 1,300 (including 170 troops on training missions), and a budget of $278 million.[112] AFRICOM has in recent years also taken a close interest in training local security forces in Northwest Africa in response to the increased threat al-Qaeda in the Islamic Maghreb (AQIM) poses to regional security. Between May 3-23, 2010, AFRICOM oversaw Operation FLINTLOCK, a training exercise in the Sahel involving 600 U.S. troops; 150 Europeans from France, Germany, the Netherlands, Spain, and the UK; and 400 soldiers from Burkina Faso, Chad, Mauritania, Mali, Niger, Nigeria, and Senegal.[113]

Other relevant examples include U.S. assistance to the Yemeni security forces combating al-Qaeda in the Arabian Peninsula (AQAP), with reports of several dozen American Special Forces operatives assisting the Yemenis, ostensibly in noncombatant roles such as intelligence-gathering, and U.S. and British financial assistance to train the nascent armed forces of the Transitional Federal Government of Somalia (TFG).[114]

Hostage Rescue.

The Munich disaster of September 5-6, 1972, in which 11 Israeli athletes were murdered by the Black September Organization (BSO) — nine during a botched West German police attempt to free them at Furstenfeldbruck airfield — inspired the FRG and other states to set up specialized hostage rescue teams for employment in either domestic or foreign emergencies. For example, by late 1972, the British government had prepared contingency plans earmarking a troop from the 22nd Special Air Service Regiment (22SAS) to "supplement police resources in the event of a hijacking incident at an airport in the United Kingdom."[115] Declassified British government files contain little on the development of 22SAS's counterterrorist unit (known by the codenames Snowdrop, then Pagoda), although sources show that its first exercise, Icon, took place in July 1973. An officer and a sergeant from 22SAS also accompanied GSG-9 when it stormed Lufthansa Flight-181 5 years later.[116] The formation of the U.S. Army's Delta Force in 1977 occurred after President Jimmy Carter, reacting to GSG9's success at Mogadishu, Africa, asked his advisors whether the U.S. armed forces had an equivalent unit with similar capabilities.[117]

These units require well-trained personnel able to swiftly assault a defended location to neutralize terrorists within it and to liberate their captives. Hostage rescue is an intensely dangerous activity, since there is a clear risk that gunmen may attempt to massacre their prisoners once they come under attack. Their location—a public building, an aircraft, or an oil rig—can also be rigged for explosives, primed for detonation if the authorities send in troops or police. The Mogadishu and Marseilles examples cited above show that a specialist police or gendarmerie unit can be successfully employed in hostage rescue. However, in cases when an incident takes place offshore or in a foreign country, where the terrorists are too numerous and well-equipped for a police unit, or where the hostage takers can rely on local assistance, military forces may be required to conduct a successful rescue. The military also possesses specific characteristics that make it ideally suited to fill particular roles. For example, the Royal Marines and, in particular, its Special Forces arm, the Special Boat Service (SBS), were a natural choice for British maritime counterterrorist planners in the late 1970s, because of the former's role as the Royal Navy's maritime/amphibious infantry arm, and the latter's intensive training in the hazardous and complex task of diving under combat conditions.

Declassified documents show that the Royal Marines and SBS were involved in offshore exercises around the North Sea oil fields from the summer of 1976.[118] In May 1980, the Royal Marines established a specialist unit (Commachio Company) to protect or recapture ships or oil rigs against armed opposition, although this unit's counterterrorist duties were transferred in full to M Squadron, SBS in July 1987.[119]

Military Special Forces units have been employed successfully in hostage rescue missions; these include the *Bijzondere Bijstands Eenheid* (BBE), ending two hostage crises in the Netherlands: in Glimmen in May 1977 (when a train and school were taken over by South Moluccan separatists); and Assen in March 1978 (when 70 people were taken hostage in a local government building by the same group). Recruited from the Royal Dutch Marines, the BBE freed all but two of the hostages at Glimmen, while at Assen the Marines stormed the local government offices in time to prevent the Moluccans from killing two of their captives.[120] 22SAS gained public notoriety when the Pagoda unit stormed the Iranian embassy on May 5, 1980, with the world's media filming the assault. Of the six Ahvaz gunmen, five were killed during the course of Operation NIMROD, and all but two of the 21 hostages were freed.[121]

The most spectacular external hostage-rescue mission was conducted by the IDF's *Sayeret Maktal* in June 1976, which liberated over 100 Israeli and Jewish passengers of Air France Flight 139, held by Palestinian and West German terrorists at Entebbe Airport outside Kampala, Uganda. The success of this mission was remarkable because of its complexity — it involved around 100 commandos being flown a distance of 3,800 kilometers in four C130 transport planes, supported by two Boeing 707s (one airborne command post and one hospital plane), all of which required air-to-air refueling during the mission. Furthermore, in contrast with Mogadishu the following year, in which GSG9 enjoyed the full cooperation of the Somali authorities, the Israelis had to conduct a rescue on hostile territory. Ugandan dictator Idi Amin supported the hijackers and ordered his army to protect them. In a domestic hostage situation, or one in friendly territory overseas, police or military Special Forces can count on regular security personnel to cordon off the terrorists and their captives and to also gather intelligence critical to any rescue attempt — such as the number of hostage takers, their location, and that of their victims. The Israelis were denied this cooperation in Entebbe, and a more effective Ugandan defense, not to mention mechanical failure on any of the planes, could have led to a disastrous failure similar to the U.S. effort to free their embassy hostages in Iran (Operation EAGLE CLAW) 4 years later. [122]

Clandestine Operations/Intelligence-Gathering.

One of the principal problems with deploying armed forces on MACA/MACP tasks is that they are doctrinally prepared and trained for interstate warfare, not for the hard task of identifying and tracking down terrorists who hide among the civilian populace. This has been a perennial problem for the British Army in particular, not only with its operations in Northern Ireland but also with previous conflicts such as Cyprus. The former commander of EOKA, General George Grivas, retrospectively mocked his British enemies for "hunting field mice with armoured cars."[123] British commanders in Cyprus did actually recognize the weaknesses of overt military activity. The British Army has a tradition of combining conventional operations—public patrolling, guarding likely targets for a terrorist attack, check points, etc.—with clandestine ones. These have included locally recruited countergangs such as the Q-Patrols (recruited from the Greek populace during the Cyprus Emergency), which caused EOKA more difficulties than Grivas was subsequently prepared to admit. The British Army also has a history of raising its own plain-clothes units—such as the *Keeni Meeni* patrols in Aden (1966-67)—and similar formations were extensively employed in Operation BANNER.[124]

With clandestine operations, intelligence is gathered in an unobtrusive and discreet manner, so as not to attract the target's attention. Plain-clothes military units can be involved in static or mobile surveillance—on foot or in unmarked vehicles—of suspects, their safe houses and arms caches, and can provide time-sensitive intelligence to direct military and police patrols to arrest terrorists. This was the role performed by the British Army's 14 Intelligence Company in Northern Ireland from early 1973 onward, and since April 2005, this is the remit of the Special Reconnaissance Regiment (SRR).[125] More controversially, the Army's Intelligence Corps also established the Force Research Unit (FRU) in 1980 to recruit informants among the Catholic and Protestant communities of Northern Ireland and to run agents within Republican and Loyalist terrorist groups. If the security forces are able to penetrate terrorist groups and recruit spies within their midst, then the former find it easier to contain the latter's activities and frustrate their operations. Yet such intelligence-gathering activity is fraught with ethical problems, which are discussed later.[126]

Other armies have also employed undercover units. The IDF's *Mista-Aravim* troops have been employed as part of a strategy of targeted killing against Palestinian militants,[127] while the U.S. Army established the Intelligence Support Activity (ISA) in the aftermath of the Iranian hostage crisis. ISA's successes include locating American citizens held by Hezbollah in Lebanon during the mid-1980s—although the administration of President Ronald Reagan did not use this intelligence to order a mission to rescue them— and the assistance its signals intelligence (SIGINT) specialists gave to the Italian police in January 1982, which enabled the latter to free kidnapped U.S. Brigadier General James Dozier, who was held hostage by the BR.[128]

State SIGINT agencies such as the U.S. National Security Agency (NSA) and the UK Government Communications Headquarters (GCHQ) are also involved in the interception of emails, mobile phone calls, and other communications between terrorist suspects. NSA is predominantly a military organization, whose director is a three-star officer drawn from the U.S. armed forces, and which is supported by U.S. military intelligence assets worldwide. While GCHQ is nominally overseen by the FCO, it also uses Royal Navy, RAF, and Army SIGINT units as part of its intelligence-gathering effort.[129] NSA and GCHQ cooperate closely with each other and their Canadian, Australian, and New Zealand counterparts (respectively; the Communications Security Establishment, the Defence Signals Directorate, and the Government Communications Security Bureau) in the Echelon program. Although it is officially described as directed against terrorism and organized crime, critics suspect that Echelon has also been exploited for more dubious practices, such as commercial espionage. Nonetheless, it is clear that Western SIGINT services have been active against terrorist groups, although given the sheer volume of intercepted traffic — around 1.3 billion email users worldwide send a daily total of approximately 210 billion messages — and limitations on the ability of agencies to collate and assess such material (in particular, the limited number of linguists and translators NSA, GCHQ, and other services employ) the SIGINT process is not as efficient as it is portrayed in Hollywood thrillers. Furthermore, official secrecy prevents an accurate assessment of the extent to which SIGINT enables Western states to thwart terrorist plots, although it is apparent that until a leak in the American media in August 1998, the NSA had a tap on one of bin Laden's satellite phones.[130]

Preemptive Intervention.

The clandestine units discussed above can also assist operations to apprehend terrorists on the verge of committing an attack. In Northern Ireland, 14 Intelligence Company provided surveillance support to 22SAS, which, alongside the RUC's Headquarters Mobile Support Unit, would intercept PIRA members on active service. 22SAS killed around 40 members of PIRA during Operation BANNER, but arrested a further 100, thereby belying Republican propaganda claims that 22SAS operated according to a shoot-to-kill policy.[131] The increasing reliance on preemptive intervention by the British Army and the RUC can be seen in the outcome of security force ambushes — nine Republican terrorists were killed by such means prior to 1983, and 35 were shot between this year and 1997. The two most effective operations were the ambush of a PIRA unit in the process of attacking the RUC station at Loughgall on May 8, 1987, during which 22SAS shot dead eight armed members of PIRA's East Tyrone Brigade; and the arrest of a 4-man sniper team in South Armagh by SAS soldiers in April 1997.[132]

Given the fact that from the mid-1970s onward PIRA numbered around 300-400 active members at most, these killings and arrests had a disproportionate effect. Furthermore, as Ed Moloney notes, the Loughgall ambush was followed up by a series of undercover Army operations that led to further losses for PIRA's Tyrone Brigade (renowned as the most hard-line of Provisional units); 28 of its members were killed in security force ambushes between May 1987 and February 1992. The shooting of PIRA volunteers in preemptive operations, most notoriously the Gibraltar killings of March 1998, did contribute to Republican propaganda demonizing the SAS, but these operations also had a demoralizing effect on the Provisionals and contributed to the ceasefire PIRA's leadership declared in July 1997.[133]

A more recent example includes the use of American and British Special Forces units, including 22SAS, to disrupt Sunni and Shia insurgent activity in Baghdad, notably the suicide and car-bomb attacks committed by al-Qaeda in Iraq (AQI). On completing his tour as the commander of multinational forces in Iraq in August 2008, General David Petraeus explicitly praised the efforts of Special Forces in crippling AQI activity in the Iraqi capital, stating that this contributed to the decline in terrorist and internecine violence in Baghdad which followed the surge of U.S. troops from February 2007.[134]

Targeted Killing.

For the purposes of this paper, the distinction between targeted killing and preemptive intervention missions that have ended lethally (such as the Northern Ireland examples noted above) needs to be emphasized. As Cronin states, "[naming] individuals and ordering their assassination is different from killing an enemy while he is engaged in an attack." From a purely legal perspective, assassinations are illegal, since they involve extrajudicial killing, but in conventional warfare, it is permissible to kill key figures within an enemy's command structure. Examples include the failed attack by British commandos on General Erwin Rommel's headquarters in Libya in November 1941, and the interception and destruction of Admiral Isoroku Yamamoto's transport plane by American fighter planes in April 1943 during the Pacific war.[135] During the early phases of Operation IRAQ FREEDOM from March-April 2003, Coalition forces tried to kill Saddam Hussein by bombing his suspected hideouts, while the British military ordered an air strike on a house in Basra that was (wrongly) identified as the headquarters for Ali Hasan al-Majid, in charge of the defense of Southern Iraq.[136] If states treat counterterrorism from a warfighting perspective, a strategy of decapitation is simply an extension of existing practice in interstate conflict.

Since 9/11, both the Bush and Obama administrations have conducted targeted strikes against their adversaries. This contentious policy is evident not only with the air strikes by Predator UAVs against al-Qaeda suspects and TTP leaders in the FATA,[137] but also in other cases such as the UAV strike on Qaid Sunyan Ali al-Harithi (a senior al-Qaeda terrorist) in Yemen on November 3, 2002, and the helicopter gunship attack on a convoy carrying Saleh Ali Saleh Nabhan in Somalia on September 15, 2009.[138] The underlying calculation behind a targeted-killing strategy is that the elimination of key leadership and support figures (notably bomb makers and financiers) can have a critical effect in weakening a terrorist group. In this respect, U.S. and Pakistani officials hoped that the death of TTP leader Baitullah Mehsud in a Predator strike in South Waziristan on August 8, 2009, would create a damaging rift within this organization, although despite an apparent bout of infighting among rival TTP commanders, these expectations remain unfulfilled.[139] The effect of such strikes on the morale of the rank and file of militants in Pakistan, Yemen, and elsewhere remains to be seen, although there is anecdotal evidence to suggest that UAV attacks have had a demoralizing effect on some survivors.[140]

The Israelis have also been consistent practitioners of this tactic, historically, against organizations such as the Palestinian Islamic Jihad (PIJ). Targeted killings have been conducted beyond Israel's borders by both military units and the Mossad.[141] Examples involving the IDF include the raid on Beirut, Lebanon, in April 1973, during which the Sayeret Maktal assassinated three BSO leaders; the commando attack that killed one of Yasser Arafat's key deputies, Khalil al-Wazir, at his home in Tunis; and the death of the Hezbollah leader, Sheikh Abas Musawi, in South Lebanon in February 1992 (Musawi's vehicle convoy was intercepted and destroyed by helicopter gunships).[142] The IDF and security forces have also conducted similar actions against Palestinian militants in Gaza and the West Bank from the early 1990s, using Mista-Aravim teams, uniformed Special Forces, and air strikes (such as the one that killed Hamas's spiritual leader, Sheikh Ahmed Yassin, on March 22, 2004).[143]

Retaliation.

A state's armed forces can be used to launch retaliatory raids or strikes against either another state that has supported a terrorist group, or against a nonstate actor based within a weak or failing state. These operations are coercive in nature, since they are intended to persuade an adversary to "choose between making concessions or suffering the consequences of continuing its present course of action."[144] In the cases discussed below, retaliatory raids are intended to compel terrorist groups to desist from perpetuating further attacks and to force their state sponsors to cease assisting them.

Israeli forces conducted raids into Egypt during the early 1950s in response to attacks by the Cairo-backed Palestinian Fedayeen, and also into Jordan during the late 1960s as a retaliation against the PLO, PFLP, and other groups' attacks on Israel. The latter arguably contributed to King Hussein's decision to crack down on the Palestinian guerrilla movement's state-within-a-state in September 1970, although this also had the unintended effect of inspiring Arafat to create the BSO. It is also noteworthy that the Syrians would not permit Palestinian groups based on its soil to launch attacks directly against the "Zionist entity," insisting that any such operations be staged from Lebanon or Jordan; Syria clearly preferred that other Arab states should face the brunt of Israeli reprisals.[145] The U.S. air strikes on Libya on April 15, 1986 (Operation EL DORADO CANYON), also provide an example of retaliation against a state sponsor, as the operation was a response to the bombing of a disco in West Berlin earlier that month (frequented by U.S. military personnel), which was sponsored by Gaddafi's intelligence services.[146]

With the Turkish-Syrian crisis of October 1998, the mere threat of military intervention forced a state to cease sponsoring a terrorist group. Syria had provided a safe haven for the PKK and its leader, Abdullah Ocalan, and PKK fighters were able to use training camps in the Bekaa Valley (Lebanon being under Syrian occupation at that time). After repeated attempts to persuade Damascus to expel the PKK, the Turkish government threatened Syria with war in early October 1998, backing hostile rhetoric with military maneuvers near the Syrian border. Then-Syrian President Hafez al-Asad was fully aware that his country was diplomatically isolated and militarily weaker than Turkey (which was also a NATO member, and could count on close alliance ties with the United States and Israel). Ocalan was deported from Syria on October 9, 1998, facilitating his capture by the Turkish secret services in Kenya the following February, and the PKK were subsequently expelled from the Bekaa Valley. Success in this case derived not only from a credible military threat, but also the fact that President Asad concluded that the benefits gained from supporting the PKK were minimal compared to the risks.[147]

Examples of retaliation specifically directed against terrorist groups include the French air raids on the Bekaa Valley in October 1983, in response to a Hezbollah suicide bombing that killed 58 French paratroopers serving with the Multi-National Peacekeeping Force (MNF) in Lebanon. (A simultaneous attack on the same day, October 23, 1983, killed 241 U.S. Marines also with the MNF.)[148] In response to the

Nairobi and Dar es-Salaam attacks, the administration of President Bill Clinton ordered cruise missile attacks against al-Qaeda training camps in Afghanistan and a suspected chemical weapons plant in Sudan, on August 20, 1998 (Operation INFINITE REACH).[149] On March 1, 2008, the Colombian Army raided FARC camps in neighboring Ecuador, killing one of its senior commanders, Raul Reyes, in the process.[150] The Israelis themselves have set several precedents, including the invasion of Lebanon in April 1982, intended to destroy the PLO's Fatahland in Southern Lebanon; the July-August 2006 war against Hezbollah caused by an ambush against an IDF patrol in Northern Israel; and the December 2008-January 2009 campaign to cripple Hamas in Gaza (Operation CAST LEAD), in response to the latter's rocket attacks on Sderot and other towns in Southern Israel.[151]

Regime Change.

The final example involves an invasion to overthrow a government that either promotes terrorism or provides a safe haven to terrorist groups. The only two examples to date have both followed the 9/11 atrocities and the Bush administration's declaration of a War on Terror. The first involved the invasion of Afghanistan on October 7, 2001, and the support given by U.S. and Coalition intelligence, air, and Special Forces to the Northern Alliance against the Taliban. The latter became a target for regime change, because it had sheltered al-Qaeda since mid-1996 and provided it with a base of operations to conduct attacks on U.S. targets up until 9/11. The Taliban leader, Mullah Omar, refused U.S. demands to hand over al-Qaeda's leadership and close down its training camps, principally because his regime depended not only on bin Laden's largesse, but also on the thousands of foreigners who had come to train in Afghanistan, providing the Taliban with their most reliable and dedicated troops organized within al-Qaeda's 055 Brigade.[152] This was very much evident during the early phases of Operation ENDURING FREEDOM (October-December 2001), when a total of around 5,000 Arab, Pakistani, and other foreign soldiers proved to be more effective and dedicated fighters for the Taliban than native Afghans—who generally defected to the Coalition and the Northern Alliance once it was apparent that the latter would prevail.[153]

In much the same way that the PLO handicapped itself in Lebanon in 1982 by organizing itself along conventional military lines, thereby leaving itself to be fixed and destroyed by the IDF, al-Qaeda fighters in Afghanistan in October-November 2001 chose to fight the Northern Alliance in positional warfare and suffered heavy losses from U.S. air strikes directed by Special Forces personnel liaising with indigenous anti-Taliban forces.[154] By December 2001, al-Qaeda and its leadership had opted to disperse; hence, the flight of bin Laden, Zawahiri, and an estimated 1,000-1,500 fighters across the Afghan border into the FATA during the battle of Tora Bora in December 2001.[155] Al-Qaeda's blunder in fighting on terms that favored the American way of war should be noted, as it is extremely rare for terrorists to fight on a footing which favors regular militaries.

The second example is the Ethiopian invasion of Somalia in December 2006, which was assisted by U.S. air power. American Special Forces units from CJTF-HOA were also apparently active in supporting Ethiopian forces. The pretext for this invasion was the supposed tolerance of the Islamic Courts Union (ICU) for al-Qaeda's activities, a claim vigorously disputed by the ICU itself. In much the same way that Operation ENDURING FREEDOM led to U.S. and allied forces being involved in a complex stabilization mission that deteriorated into an insurgency against a resurgent Taliban, Ethiopia's intervention drew it into a debilitating conflict in Somalia that lasted until it withdrew its troops in January 2009.[156] Both cases show the limitations of military force as a counterterrorist tool, discussed in more detail in the next sections.

PROBLEMS ARISING FROM MILITARY INVOLVEMENT IN COUNTERTERRORISM — THE INTERNATIONAL CONTEXT

The previous section shows that in a variety of scenarios, armed forces can be employed both to support a state's counterterrorist policies and also to provide capabilities which civilian agencies (such as the police and the intelligence services) may lack. For example, with Operation FLAVIUS in March 1988, soldiers from the 22SAS were sent to Gibraltar by the British government because the local police force lacked the trained personnel required to arrest the PIRA terrorists, who were planning a bomb attack on the peninsula. Military personnel often also have the physical and psychological stamina needed to operate in hostile environments bereft of the comforts that Western civilians take for granted, which makes them, and in particular Special Forces operatives, a tempting asset for policymakers envisaging a decisive strike against overseas terrorist groups and sanctuaries.[157]

Given the can-do attitude that is a characteristic of Western militaries, and also the fact that their personnel are prepared to endure considerable hardship and risk to life and limb as part of their profession, there is a clear temptation for governments to treat their armed forces as a magic bullet for solving complex problems. Yet, as the BBC journalist Hugh Sykes noted, the military often deals with symptoms, not causes, and the same can be said of counterterrorism.[158] There are several potential pitfalls of employing military means to fight terrorism in the international arenas listed below. Those dealing with domestic counterterrorism are examined in the following section. These issues are often interlinked and should not be considered in isolation.

Cooperation with Local Security Forces.

One of the first risks a state runs when providing military personnel to assist allied forces in counterterrorist training is that its own soldiers can become targets for attack. In February 2010, three U.S. servicemen working with the Pakistani Frontier Corps died in a bombing in the NWFP (two schoolgirls were also killed in this attack).[159] Second, the ability of Western troops to interact effectively with indigenous personnel can vary. American counterterrorist cooperation with the Armed Forces of the Philippines (AFP) is facilitated by decades of contacts between an Anglophone AFP and the U.S. armed forces. An *Economist* journalist writing on this relationship noted that American and Filipino service personnel regular bonded off-duty over a few beers and a karaoke session, wryly observing that such a technique might not work with Yemeni soldiers. AFRICOM's exercise in the Sahel in May 2010 (Operation FLINTLOCK) experienced certain practical difficulties, most notably regarding the fact that nearly all the African personnel involved were Francophone; the challenges of translating remarks by U.S. instructors were compounded by the difficulties in finding French phases for specific military terms, such as "a contact."[160]

Third, there are few guarantees that training missions can prevent local security force personnel from going rogue, or from conducting themselves in a manner that discredits both the host nation and its Western ally (or allies). Operation MONOGRAM, the British MOD's program for training foreign armies in counterterrorist tactics, received negative press scrutiny in July 2008 that focused on the Kenyan Army's elite unit, 20 Para. This British-trained formation has been accused of numerous human rights abuses against civilians in its operations against the Sabaot Land Defence Force, a militant group active near the Ugandan border. For media critics, the abuses allegedly committed by 20 Para were reminiscent of the atrocities committed by the British colonial forces during the Mau Mau uprising in Kenya of 1952-57.[161]

As Daniel Byman notes, the task of training indigenous police and military forces to fight both terrorists and insurgents is fraught with problems. States beset by terrorism or guerrilla violence are in certain cases poorly governed and administered, and local security forces can be inadequately trained and equipped. A lack of professionalism—not to mention the tendency of some governments to coup-proof their regimes by creating parallel paramilitary forces, dividing the armed forces' chain of command, or by promoting commanders on the basis of loyalty rather than competence—means that Western military trainers are often hampered in their efforts to establish professional and effective security forces.[162] There is also a risk that elite units trained and funded by the United States and other Western countries might be used by auto-cratic governments to suppress dissent and to crush political opposition. The former Pakistani military dictator, General Pervez Musharraf, used U.S. aid in-tended to fight extremists in the FATA against insur-gents in Baluchistan. Funds that had been provided to help the Pakistani Army against Islamist terrorists were instead used to crush a nationalist movement unconnected with al-Qaeda or the TTP. Regarding Ye-men and its own internal problems, the government of President Al Abdullah Saleh is far more concerned with the rebellion by the Houthi tribesmen and South-ern separatists than with AQAP. It is therefore likely that U.S. and British assistance to the Yemeni security forces will not actually be employed for the purposes intended by the donors.[163]

The dilemma for Western governments is that regional allies such as Pakistan and Uzbekistan are perceived to be of such strategic importance that state failure could have disastrous consequences for re-gional and international security; this is, of course, a particularly frightening prospect in a nuclear-armed Pakistan.[164] This supposition is based on the debat-able proposition that these states are on the verge of collapse. Furthermore, by funding and arming indig-enous security forces, external supporters become automatically linked with human rights abuses and atrocities committed by the former, thereby becom-ing the focus of both international criticism and local resentment. President Karimov's egregious despotism and corruption is an affront to civilized values, but Uzbekistan's provision of host-nation logistical sup-port for the NATO mission in Afghanistan makes him a necessary ally as far as Western governments are concerned. Karimov also has leverage over his Western sponsors, as demonstrated in the aftermath of the Andijan massacre on May 13, 2005, in which hundreds of anti-government demonstrators were gunned down by his security forces. The Uzbek government responded to State Department condemnation of this atrocity by ordering American military personnel out of the Karshi-Khanabad air base on July 29; the base had been leased to the United States in the aftermath of 9/11. Karimov showed the United States and other Western powers that he was in a position to respond to criticisms of his domestic record by hampering NATO's war effort against the Taliban.[165] It is therefore not surprising that Western governments have continued to tolerate Uzbekistan's abominable human rights record as the price to pay for its support for the troubled mission in Afghanistan, and, indeed, U.S. defense cooperation with Tashkent was subsequently resumed in early 2010.[166]

A further problem, common to COIN as well, is that the security forces of local allies can become infiltrated with terrorist sympathizers and informants, not to mention various other undesirable elements. During the British military occupation of Basra from 2003-09, the local police was heavily infiltrated by militias and insurgents, and became a compromised force heavily involved in organized crime, political feuding, and anti-coalition attacks.[167] A similar problem affects U.S. and allied policy toward Pakistan, insofar as the Pakistani Army and its intelligence wing (Inter-Services Intelligence [ISI]) have an unknown number of personnel who support the ideology of the Afghan Taliban and its Pakistani counterparts in the FATA.[168] The shortcomings of the Frontier Corps in fighting the Taliban in the FATA became evident in 2006-07. Not only was this paramilitary force poorly trained and equipped, but many of its ethnic Pashtun soldiers sympathized with the Taliban militants they were fighting.[169]

Police training is often the weak link in Western aid programs to indigenous security forces. It is the police who provide a direct link with the population, maintaining law and order and the writ of the government. They are of crucial importance in both COIN and counterterrorism because they are familiar with the local environment and provide a permanent presence amongst the civilian population. Yet, as current experience with the Iraqi Police Service (IPS) and the Afghan National Police (ANP) shows, police training is often a secondary priority to the training of local militaries, despite the fact that it is as important to create an effective constabulary as it is to raise an army. Furthermore, the culture/experience gap dividing Western police advisors (and military police trainers) from their indigenous recruits needs to be borne in mind. A U.S. civil affairs officer noted with reference to his experiences in Vietnam in 1973 that "[cement] police weren't able to advise rice-paddy cops," and these differences between developed and Third World policing need to be considered in any program training *souq* or *arbakai* cops today.[170]

Practicality.

In some scenarios, notably hostage rescue, counterterrorist operations can be thwarted by either a lack of host-nation support or even by local authorities cooperating with the terrorists. A prime example was the takeover of TWA Flight 847 on June 14, 1985, by Hezbollah. U.S. efforts to free the hostages with a military operation became impossible once the hijacked plane landed in Beirut and the crew and passengers were dispersed across the city.[171] On December 25, 1999, Indian Airlines Flight 814 was hijacked by *Harkat ul-Mujadidin* (HUM), a Pakistani group involved in the Kashmiri insurgency, which also had close links with the Taliban and al-Qaeda. The plane was flown to Kandahar, and the hijackers and their hostages were guarded by the Taliban regime. A rescue mission was therefore impossible, and so the Indian government was forced to concede to HUM's demands and release its leader, Maulana Masud Azhar, and two other members from prison.[172]

On April 24, 1980, the Carter administration attempted to send a rescue force to liberate the U.S. diplomats held hostage by the Iranian revolutionary regime following the embassy takeover on November 4, 1979. In retrospect, this was very much a "Mission: Impossible," and its failure had more to do with the sheer scale of the challenge faced by the planners than any shortcomings within the U.S. military. Operation EAGLE CLAW involved flying a combined Delta Force/U.S. Army Ranger group 1,500 kilometers from Masirah air-base in Oman to a clandestine location in Iran (known as Desert One). U.S. military commanders rejected bases in Turkey for fear that the Soviets might pick up the helicopter and C130 flights by radar and alert the revolutionary regime. The rescue force was then to drive and helicopter to Tehran to storm the embassy and free the captives, making its escape from the Iranian capital right under the noses of the local security forces, not to mention the various militias that had emerged in the aftermath of Ayatollah Khomeini's seizure of power. As one Delta Force officer quipped, the only difference between Operation EAGLE CLAW and the Alamo was that "Davy Crockett didn't have to fight his way in." The attempted rescue mission was aborted by President Jimmy Carter while it was assembling at Desert One, and eight U.S. servicemen were killed when a helicopter collided with a C130. Yet it can be argued that the Americans were lucky; if Carter had not aborted Operation EAGLE CLAW, there could well have been catastrophically high casualties among the commandos and also the embassy staff. The harsh fact was that nothing short of a full-scale military invasion of Iran, with all the diplomatic and political consequences involved, could have worked, and even in this instance it is likely that the Iranians would have murdered their captives well before they could have been rescued.[173]

Even in cases where host governments are not collaborating with terrorists, petty politics can hamper hostage rescue missions. During the Munich crisis of September 5, 1972, the Federal German government rejected Israeli appeals to send a *Sayeret Maktal* team to free the athletes held by the BSO, relying instead on the Bavarian police. While the Israeli army Special Forces had one successful hostage rescue mission to their credit (with the storming of Sabena Flight 571 at Lod airport on May 9, 1972), the Bavarian state police had no counterterrorist experience whatsoever. The grisly consequences of this decision were seen on the runway of Furstenfeldbruck the following morning. On November 23, 1985, the ANO hijacked EgyptAir Flight 648 en route from Athens to Cairo, diverting the plane to Luqa Airport, Malta. The Maltese government turned down American offers to send Delta Force to storm the plane, pleading neutrality, and turned instead to its Egyptian counterpart, Force 777. The Egyptian commandos bungled the November 25th rescue mission, provoking a firefight in which

56 out of 88 passengers were killed.[174] In both cases, a high price was paid for observing political niceties.

Retaliatory missions can also be unfeasible if state sponsors are strong enough to escalate in response. For example, throughout the Cold War it was impossible for Western countries or Israel to take any action against the USSR or other Warsaw Pact states (such as the GDR or Czechoslovakia) that offered assistance to the PLO or to far-left European terrorist groups. Iran's implicit threat to unleash Hezbollah, Hamas, and other proxies, not to mention to increase assistance to anti-Coalition forces in Iraq and Afghanistan, is such that the United States, Israel, and other European countries are unwilling to use military means to coerce Tehran.[175] As noted below, the Indians face a similar problem regarding Pakistan's sponsorship of groups (such as LET and HUM) involved since 1989 in the insurgency in Kashmir.

Military Reluctance.

A further obstacle to the involvement of armed forces in counterterrorism is the unwillingness of military chiefs to become involved. For example, after the U.S. Marine barracks bombing in Beirut in October 1983, the U.S. Defense Secretary Caspar Weinberger, with the support of the Joint Chiefs of Staff (JCS), barred retaliatory strikes against IR positions in the Bekaa Valley. In the aftermath of the Vietnam War, and following the adoption of an all-volunteer force in 1973, the U.S. Army focused its training, organization, and doctrine on the challenges of interstate warfare (with the USSR and Warsaw Pact until the end of the Cold War, and then with potential adversaries such as Iraq, Iran, and North Korea from 1990). Counterterrorism, alongside other missions such as peacekeeping and COIN, has been traditionally viewed by the U.S. military hierarchy as a distraction from missions more important to the national interest.[176] Even in the post-9/11 environment, there is still a pronounced concern among U.S. Army officers that a force which focuses too much on fighting irregular foes will lose the ability to fight so-called proper wars, and that the U.S. military risks a disastrous defeat if called upon to wage a conventional war against a state-based adversary.[177]

During the Clinton administration, the JCS proved to be particularly reluctant warriors. The chiefs repeatedly provided a negative response to White House queries about the feasibility of sending U.S. Special Forces units to capture bin Laden in Afghanistan during 1998-99, stating that such raids were militarily impossible. The chiefs were correct in this assessment; operations in Afghanistan since October 2001 show that such military operations cannot be conducted without the support of neighboring powers, and without a massive commitment in terms of manpower and logistical resources. However, critics of the JCS argued that the military hierarchy was also affected by an excessive timidity concerning losses (deemed the "body bag" mentality), and also the widespread distrust and dislike for the Clinton administration within the U.S. armed forces. The failure of the Somalia peacekeeping mission from 1992-93 impressed upon the JCS the suspicion that the White House would order them into ill-defined, insufficiently resourced, and complicated tasks, and would dodge responsibility if missions went awry and military personnel were killed.[178]

Although the British armed forces have a more sustained record of involvement in counterterrorism, not to mention COIN, there is also evident disquiet within the UK's military hierarchy concerning the current operational focus on the War on Terror. Prior to his retirement, former head of the British Army General Sir Richard Dannatt suggested that Afghanistan and other commitments may sap the Army's ability to conduct high-intensity military operations and maneuver warfare. The Royal Navy is also concerned that its current involvement in anti-piracy and Operation ACTIVE ENDEAVOUR-type missions may result in "skills fade," particularly in areas of maritime warfare relevant to interstate conflict such as antisubmarine warfare.[179]

"Pin-Pricks" — The Perception of Ineffectiveness.

Retaliatory strikes may have a counterproductive effect if they are judged — not least by the targets themselves — to be ineffective. Operation INFINITE REACH failed to kill bin Laden, and therefore enabled the latter to present himself to fellow Muslims as someone who had defied a superpower and survived the consequences.[180] For its part, the U.S. media automatically linked the cruise missile strikes on Afghanistan and Sudan with Clinton's forthcoming impeachment by Congress over his affair with Monica Lewinsky. Operation INFINITE REACH was greeted by comparisons with a Hollywood satire in which a fictional President, beset by a sex scandal, concocts an artificial war to distract media attention and to exploit the patriotic response from the American public. When Secretary of Defense William Cohen faced a press conference after the missile strikes, one of the first questions asked was whether President Clinton had been inspired by the film, *Wag the Dog*.[181]

Clinton did recognize that the use of precision weapons would be interpreted not as discrimination, but as cowardice, by bin Laden and his followers. The apparent unwillingness of Americans to risk the lives of troops in raids on al-Qaeda camps contributed to bin Laden's propaganda claims that the United States was weak, and that its soldiers lacked the courage to fight. Conscious of this potential reaction, Clinton apparently cornered Chairman of the JCS General Hugh Shelton after a National Security Council (NSC) meeting on August 17, 1998, (following the decision to launch Operation INFINITE REACH) to suggest the following:

> Hugh, what I think would scare the shit out of these al-Qaeda guys more than any cruise missile . . . would be the sight of U.S. commandos, Ninja guys in black suits, jumping out of helicopters into their camps, spraying machine guns. Even if we don't get the big guys, it will have a good effect.[182]

Clinton's unfamiliarity with the practicalities of military operations is evident here, but he also displayed a fairly accurate understanding of his enemies' psyche.

Related weaknesses can be identified in military operations on the ground, sometimes as a consequence of inflated expectations and government spin. Following the clash between U.S. forces and al-Qaeda fighters in Operation ANACONDA in March 2002, a multinational task force was sent into Southeastern Afghanistan (Operation JACANA) the following month, its mission being to "destroy the terrorist infrastructure in South-East Afghanistan." The bulk of this force came from 45 Commando Royal Marines, and prior to JACANA, the British government informed the media that a major battle was imminent. The failure of the Royal Marines to actually confront al-Qaeda fighters in combat was therefore treated by the press as evidence that the mission was a failure, notwithstanding the fact that al-Qaeda retreated and denied 45 Commando a chance to engage and destroy them.[183]

The third Israeli invasion of Lebanon from July 13-August 14, 2006, also highlighted the problem of inflated expectations. It was counterproductive not merely because of the civilian casualties caused by IDF air strikes (these, apparently, involved 1,191 killed and 4,409 injured), but also because the air-centric campaign was treated by Hezbollah's propaganda as evidence of Israeli unwillingness to fight the IR face-to-face. IDF Chief of Staff Air Force Lieutenant General Dan Halutz contributed further damage to the Israeli war effort by proclaiming that air strikes alone would destroy Hezbollah's missile sites and cripple the IR. In fact, Israeli ground troops had to be committed on July 23 to engage Hezbollah's fighters in close-quarter combat. Although the IR apparently lost around 500 dead (to 121 IDF personnel), Hezbollah hailed the outcome of the conflict as a "divine and strategic victory," with Sheikh Hasan Nasrallah gloating about "the Zionists' failure to defeat us."[184] On the Israeli side, there was widespread public criticism of Ehud Olmert's government, reflecting the general view that Israel had lost because of its failure to destroy the IR. The Lebanon war was therefore judged by regional opinion to have damaged the credibility of Israel's deterrence strategy, and to have had the same effect on Hezbollah as the Karameh clash of February 15, 1968, (an indecisive and costly IDF cross-border raid into Jordan that gave its target, Fatah, wider regional prestige for standing up to "the Zionists").

The "Bully Effect" — The Ethical Aspect of a Military Response.

Paradoxically, military retaliation can also arouse international and domestic criticism, and claims that the states involved are resorting to disproportionate and indiscriminate violence. This partly arises from the problems involved in acquiring accurate intelligence identifying the perpetrators of any terrorist atrocity, not to mention their sponsors, and then of using such information to justify a retaliatory strike. With Operation EL DORADO CANYON in April 1986, the United States could not reveal that it could link Libyan intelligence to the West Berlin disco bombing through SIGINT intercepts, so air strikes on Libya were regarded even by U.S. NATO allies, with the exception of the UK, as unjustified. This problem becomes a more significant one for democratic states if there are substantial civilian casualties, which almost invariably occur as a consequence of retaliatory operations.[185]

The Laws of Armed Conflict (LOAC) stress that states do have a right to resort to military action (known as *jus ad bellum*), provided that in the process they can demonstrate **just cause** (notably the requirements of self defense: lawful authority; right intention; that they act in proportion to the injury received; have a reasonable chance of success; and are using force as a **last resort**. An examination of the U.S. attack on Afghanistan shows how contentious these principles are in practice. The Bush administration could claim **just cause** because al-Qaeda had attacked the United States, and the Taliban were complicit insofar as they had granted it a sanctuary in Afghanistan and considerable influence over the country. The Americans had no United Nations Security Council (UNSC) resolu-

71

tion endorsing Operation ENDURING FREEDOM, but acted with the implicit approval of fellow permanent members of the Security Council, and indeed nearly all United Nations (UN) member states. The UNSC had already issued a resolution (SCR1267) on October 15, 1999, demanding that the Taliban cease assisting and sheltering al-Qaeda, and the passage of SCR1373 on September 28, 2001, and SCR1378 on November 14, 2001, implicitly legitimized the U.S.-led effort to overthrow Mullah Omar's regime. Although some governments insist that Article 51 only applies to attacks from states, in the case of Afghanistan there was a near-universal consensus that al-Qaeda and the Taliban were *de facto* aggressors after 9/11.[186]

Critics argue that war was not a **last resort** because the Bush administration did not engage in a diplomatic alternative, such as to persuade the Taliban to hand over bin Laden for trial. Proponents of military action convincingly argue that such an effort would have been futile given the dependence of Mullah Omar's regime on al-Qaeda, and that supposed Taliban attempts to negotiate with the United States prior to October 7, 2001, constituted a cynical effort to play for time. U.S. diplomats had, after all, repeatedly tried to persuade the Taliban to give up bin Laden before 9/11, and the Taliban's response to President Bush's demands to hand over al-Qaeda's leadership and close its training camps were a repetition of the bad faith and equivocations Mullah Omar's envoys had offered over the past 3 years.[187] **Right intention** can be judged to be in contention with **proportionality;** if the latter is considered to be more important than the former, then the Afghan civilian losses caused by the war outweigh the intention of the United States and its allies to remove al-Qaeda from Afghanistan and to promote a post-Taliban government, which is representative of all ethnic groups and can maintain peace and security within Afghanistan's borders. As for the question of whether the U.S.-led intervention had **a reasonable chance of success**, the insurgency by a revived Taliban movement is considered by critics of the war as proof that the United States, Britain, and other states involved in the conflict had no justification for thinking that a successful outcome was feasible. An alternative argument is that it was the Western Coalition's objectives, such as democratization, rather than the intervention which lacked feasibility.[188]

Critics of military reprisals — whether governments, nongovernmental organizations (NGOs) or the media — can employ double standards. Both the Israeli invasion of Lebanon in 2006 and the Gaza war of December 2008-January 2009 aroused international condemnation of the casualties that ensued (with reference to the latter, Palestinian sources claimed that 926 civilians were killed), not to mention frequent allegations of IDF war crimes. In contrast, the latter phases of the Sri Lankan Army offensive against the LTTE in May 2009 attracted far less censure. The UN's Human Rights Council was vocal about the former, but made no complaint about the latter.[189] The Israeli government also issued furious protests when the Human Rights Council's Fact Finding Mission, chaired by the South African Judge Richard Goldstone, issued its report on September 15, 2009, claiming that the report placed insufficient emphasis on Hamas's own conduct during the Gaza war.[190]

Certain claims about the humanitarian consequences of retaliatory strikes also need to be examined with care. Chomsky asserts that the U.S. cruise missile strike on the al-Shifa plant in Sudan on August

20 destroyed half of that country's pharmaceutical supplies, and that this "one bombing, according to the estimates made by the German Embassy in Sudan and Human Rights Watch (HRW), probably led to tens of thousands of deaths." In fact, neither the HRW nor the German diplomatic service had produced any such estimates. Chomsky also failed to explain how any source could produce such a precise assessment on civilian losses within a state which, at the time he was writing, was still undergoing a bloody civil war.[191] A further example involves the IDF operation to clear the West Bank town of Jenin of Palestinian militants in response to a series of suicide bombings in Israel (April 2-11, 2002). Palestinian claims that the Israeli military were involved in a wholesale slaughter of hundreds of civilians continue to circulate on the Internet, despite an HRW report showing that this massacre did not take place.[192]

One of the first problems with military strikes involves the utility of intelligence. The Clinton administration targeted the al-Shifa plant as part of Operation INFINITE REACH because of inaccurate intelligence indicating that it was owned by bin Laden, and that chemical weapons were being produced there. At the NSC meeting on August 17, 1998, opinions were evidently swayed when Clinton's National Security Advisor, Sandy Berger, asked "What if we do not hit [the al-Shifa factory] and then, after an attack, nerve gas is released in the New York City subway? What will we say then?"[193] The Israeli record of retaliatory raids into the Palestinian territories and the West Bank, not to mention the closing phases of the Sri Lankan civil war and the MACP examples discussed subsequently, also illustrate the severe challenges of identifying and targeting terrorists and militants who fight from within the midst of a wider civilian population.[194] As with COIN in general, if armed forces kill large numbers of irregular adversaries, but also cause substantial civilian losses, then this military success is ultimately a counterproductive one, since it can mobilize popular support toward the insurgent/terrorist cause.

A final issue here, particularly evident regarding the Gaza war, is the issue of proportionality. The UN Human Rights Council and NGOs such as HRW asserted that the IDF campaign against Hamas (Operation CAST LEAD) was a disproportionate response, and essentially involved the collective punishment of the 1.5 million Palestinians in Gaza. The Israeli government's response was that it was obliged to act in self-defense, as Hamas and other militant groups were firing Qassam rockets from Gaza at civilians in Southern Israel. The Israelis also acted on the basis that a strictly proportionate response to the Qassams—namely, reprisal air or ground raids on suspected launch sites—would not deter continued attacks against their people.[195] A proportionate response would therefore be less effective than an overwhelming military response that forced the Hamas leadership into stopping Qassam strikes against Southern Israel. Given the reduced rate of rocket attacks from Gaza in the aftermath of Operation CAST LEAD, Israeli officials can claim that (in the short term) the IDF assault on Hamas was actually an effective response.[196]

Political Sensitivities.

Military action can be blocked by wider political considerations, as demonstrated by the U.S. Government's repeated efforts between August 1998 and September 2001 to kill bin Laden with a cruise missile strike. The task was already a complicated one because intelligence on the al-Qaeda leader's whereabouts was time-sensitive, and because of the time period required for the Tomahawk missiles on U.S. Navy submarines to be prepared for firing. On at least two occasions in 1999, the order to strike was not given by the Clinton administration for fear of substantial civilian casualties amongst Afghans. Reports of a desert camp being constructed were received by Washington, DC, in February 1999, and initial CIA assessments were that it was being prepared for bin Laden. However, the CIA subsequently received reports that the camp was for some princes from the United Arab Emirates (UAE) present in Afghanistan on a hunting trip. Rather than taking the risk of missing bin Laden — while incinerating members of the royal family of an allied power — the Clinton administration decided to abort the planned strike.[197]

Fears of military retaliation may block international cooperation against terrorism. One example was Riyadh's response to the Khobar Towers bombing of June 25, 1996, that killed 19 American servicemen. The attack was linked to an Iranian-supported group recruited from the kingdom's Shia minority; yet the Saudi authorities refused to assist the FBI's investigation into the attack, apparently for fear that the United States, once it had proof of Tehran's complicity, would launch reprisal attacks on Iran.[198]

In the aftermath of 9/11, U.S. drone strikes in the Middle East and Pakistan have had profound political implications. While regional governments may privately sanction and, in the case of the Pakistanis, actually provide base rights and intelligence to the Americans, the popular reaction to UAV attacks places U.S. allies under severe pressure. The Yemeni government acquiesced in the strike that killed Qaid al-Harithi in November 2002, up until the point where then-Secretary of Defense Donald Rumsfeld publicly announced the U.S. role in his death; once American involvement was no longer plausibly deniable, the regime in Sanaa was forced by Yemeni public opinion to condemn the UAV strike. The reported killing of Rashid Rauf in a drone attack on November 21, 2008, also caused problems for Anglo-American relations. Rauf, wanted in connection with the thwarted plot to bomb transatlantic airliners in August 2006, had British citizenship, and reports of his death were greeted with considerable unease by the Labour government, which was conscious of the hostile reaction that UAV attacks in the FATA arouses among the one million British citizens of Pakistani descent.[199] The Pakistani government, for its part, faced popular resentment that the country has been dragged into "Washington's war." Pakistani civilian and military officials are also becoming increasingly hostile toward Western accusations that they are not doing enough to fight terrorism, most notably with reference to the Afghan Taliban's havens in Pakistan, pointing out that Pakastani armed forces have suffered thousands of casualties in their war against the TTP.[200]

Diplomatic Consequences.

Specific military measures may be treated by other states as a threat to their own national interests and can cause diplomatic implications. The establishment of AFRICOM as a U.S. military regional command has aroused a generally wary response from African states, hence the fact that its headquarters is still based in Stuttgart, Germany. Nigerian officials suspect that it is a means of undercutting their country's regional influence, while the South African government has expressed concerns that AFRICOM will destabilize the continent by embroiling it in the War on Terror, thereby undermining the African Union. Academic critics also portray AFRICOM as a Trojan Horse for U.S. neocolonialism, and as a cover for its commercial, economic, and strategic competition with China and other powers that are developing their own stake in exploiting the continent's resources.[201]

Some of the sensitivity surrounding AFRICOM can be seen with Operation FLINTLOCK. U.S. officials were quick to deny claims that the exercise had more to do with satisfying American objectives — notably reconnaissance for future intervention missions in West Africa — than with the training requirements of the African troops involved. Algeria refused to take part in Operation FLINTLOCK and has made its own efforts to combat AQIM with regional partners, including the establishment of a joint military command with Mali, Mauritania, and Niger based at Tamanrasset. Algerian suspicions of U.S. intentions in the region may prove to be a significant barrier to multilateral cooperation against AQIM.[202]

U.S. military assistance to the former Soviet republics of Georgia, Armenia, and Azerbaijan also carries with it significant diplomatic risks, given not only the authoritarian nature of the regimes concerned, but the fact that all three states are embroiled in intractable disputes over territory and separatism — Armenia and Azerbaijan over Nagorno-Karabakh, Georgia with the self-declared republics of South Ossetia and Abkhazia (both backed by Moscow, with the former being the *casus belli* of the war of August 2008). American training and equipment may therefore be employed by its recipients in these frozen conflicts, rather than for counterterrorism.[203]

Even in a domestic context, military action can affect relations with neighbors, particularly if troops cross international borders either accidentally or as part of a policy of hot pursuit. During Operation BANNER, the poorly demarcated border between the UK and Eire led to a series of Anglo-Irish squabbles arising whenever the Irish police (*Garda Siochana*) and armed forces discovered British troops on the wrong side of the frontier. These incidents generally arose from navigational errors, notably when two carloads of plain-clothes soldiers from 22SAS were arrested by the *Garda* on May 5, 1976, but they also aroused suspicions on both sides of the border that British assassination squads were slipping across the border to murder PIRA suspects living in the Irish Republic.[204] According to BBC journalist Mark Urban, a major incident was narrowly avoided during the late 1970s when a patrol of British paratroopers was landed in error by an RAF helicopter within Eire, and almost ended up in a firefight with the Irish Army. If Urban's story is true, it represented a rare lapse in the cooperative, albeit discreet, relationship between the police and military forces that both states developed from the early 1970s onward. Close Anglo-Irish cross-border contacts ensured that accidental British incursions did not have wider political repercussions on bilateral relations.[205]

With Operation BANNER, the British government was dealing with a counterpart with which it had generally friendly relations. The same could not be said with Turkey and the Kurdish Regional Government (KRG) in Northern Iraq. During the 1990s, when Iraqi Kurdistan emerged as a de facto independent state, the PKK used Northern Iraq as a sanctuary in its military campaign against the Turkish state, and the Turkish military conducted cross-border reprisal raids in 1995 and 1999. In the aftermath of the Anglo-American invasion of Iraq (March-April 2003), the Turkish General Staff and nationalist politicians feared that the KRG would secede from the Iraqi state and provide the focus for a successful Kurdish secessionist campaign in Southeastern Turkey. The existence of PKK bases in Northern Iraq was therefore not only a source of tension between Ankara and Irbil, but also had a negative impact on U.S.-Turkish relations. The Kurdish question had the potential to destroy Washington's relationship with one of its key regional allies, and when the Turks launched air strikes against PKK sites in Iraq in December 2007—followed by a land offensive with 10,000 troops (Operation SUN) in February 2008—Iraqi Kurdish politicians publicly declared that the Turkish General Staff's real intention was to crush the KRG, not the PKK. Since Operation SUN, the KRG's efforts to persuade Turkey that it has no pan-Kurdish agenda have eased tensions, although the PKK problem still has a potentially destabilizing effect on the quadrilateral relationship between Washington, Ankara, Baghdad, and Irbil.[206]

Making a Bad Situation Worse.

The decision to resort to military retaliation, either against terrorists located in a weak but friendly state, or against a state sponsor, can have destabilizing consequences. The IDF's strike against the BSO in Beirut in April 1973 helped intensify the communal tensions in Lebanon at that time. The Palestinians suspected the Christian-dominated government of conniving in the *Sayeret Maktal*'s commando raid. This operation was therefore one of many factors that contributed to the outbreak of the Lebanese civil war 2 years later. Israeli military intervention in 1982 also contributed to intercommunal and sectarian violence in Lebanon; the most damning example being the IDF's role in facilitating the Phalangist militia's bloody assault on the Palestinian refugee camps at Sabra and Chatilla in September of that year. While Sabra and Chatilla was one of many atrocities committed by the warring factions during the Lebanese civil war (for which their Syrian, Iranian, Iraqi, and Libyan sponsors remain complicit), Menachem Begin's Israeli government was justifiably pilloried by domestic and international opinion for allowing this massacre to occur.[207]

Aside from one Special Forces raid into South Waziristan on September 3, 2008, the Americans have avoided ground attacks across the Afghan border into the FATA, recognizing that these may well lead to a furious backlash in Pakistan, if not to clashes between U.S. and Pakistani troops.[208] President Obama has, however, continued his predecessor's policy of ordering Predator strikes in FATA, and firm figures on militant and civilian losses are difficult to obtain. Estimates vary from between 14 members of al-Qaeda and 687 Pakistani civilians killed between January 2006 and April 2009, to 865 al-Qaeda and Pakistani Taliban killed (for the loss of an additional 95 civilians) during the same period. A recent BBC estimate lists a total of 700 fatalities in UAV strikes (without differentiating between militants and civilians) since January 2009, and a further 1,800 deaths caused by militant attacks across Pakistan during the same period.[209]

The following points are worth noting: First, drone attacks have killed a number of significant militant leaders between August 2009 and July 2010, including

Baitullah Mehsud, Tahir Yuldashev (the leader of the IMU), Hussein al-Yemeni (the alleged plotter of the suicide bomb attack against a CIA outpost in Khost on December 31, 2009), and Saeed al-Masri (the commander of al-Qaeda in Afghanistan), although claims that the current TTP leader Hakimullah Mehsud was killed in February 2010 have been proven false. Second, it is impossible to independently distinguish between militant and civilian casualties after a strike because TTP fighters cordon off the scene of any attack. The FATA is also in this respect an extremely dangerous environment for any Western or Pakistani journalist or NGO activist trying to investigate the effects of drone strikes. Third, the Pakistani researcher Farhat Taj argues that Predator attacks are privately condoned by many Pashtun tribesmen, since they eliminate militants who have imposed a reign of terror across the FATA; the disadvantage being that the TTP and al-Qaeda are swift to hunt down and execute suspected informants after each UAV strike. But it is also evident that beyond the FATA, Predator attacks cause fierce resentment within Pakistani public opinion and have also led the TTP and its allies to increase their attacks against the authorities and the security forces, which they view as complicit in U.S. drone strikes. The challenge for American policymakers is to balance the tactical benefits of eliminating senior militants in the FATA with the strategic problem of ensuring Islamabad's continued engagement in a struggle against the TTP, which has led to several thousand military and civilian casualties (the latter arising mainly from suicide bombings which have intensified since the Pakistani Army's offensive into the FATA). While the vast majority of Pakistanis have no sympathy for the Taliban, they are also sensitive to the civilian losses and infringements of sovereignty that drone strikes entail; thus the United States risks beating the TTP and other Islamist militants in an unpopularity contest.[210]

The Predator strikes raise a further dilemma concerning the efficacy of decapitation attacks aimed at a terrorist group's leadership. While military and civilian bureaucracies may run the risk of mirror-imaging in assuming that the death or incapacitation of key leaders in a terrorist organization will have a crippling effect on the latter's operations, groups facing a combination of police and military pressure may adopt a more horizontal organizational structure in order to survive. Al-Qaeda has clearly become more networked and less hierarchical as a result of Operation ENDURING FREEDOM, which removed its Afghan sanctuary, not to mention global cooperation between police and intelligence services to neutralize its operatives worldwide. But as a consequence, bin Laden and Ayman al-Zawahiri have sacrificed their capability to control and direct the various branches of al-Qaeda worldwide. The most immediate by-product has been the series of atrocities against Muslims, such as those committed by AQI in Iraq since 2003, which have outraged Islamic opinion and caused a backlash against bin Laden and his cause.[211]

The Russians faced a problem similar to that of the Americans with FATA, involving the Pankisi Gorge in Georgia. The local population has ethnic ties with the Chechens, and the Gorge is described by Moscow as a sanctuary for Chechen separatists and a conduit for assistance to the insurgency in Chechnya itself. The Georgian government rejected Russian demands to station troops in Pankisi, and in the summer of 2002 the Russians threatened to invade. From Tblisi's perspective, Russia's counterterrorist policy regarding the Pankisi provides a pretext for the continued coercion of Georgia, and persistent efforts to dictate the terms of Georgian foreign policy and to force the country to remain within the Russian sphere of influence. The quarrel over Pankisi is not the sole cause of Russo-Georgian tensions, but it contributed to the decline in relations between Moscow and Tblisi, leading to war in August 2008.[212]

Military action can also have calamitous consequences if it is directed against the wrong target. This point is amply demonstrated by the manner in which the Bush administration exploited 9/11 to settle scores with Saddam Hussein, but also by the second Israeli invasion of Lebanon in April 1982. Begin and his Defence Minister, Ariel Sharon, used the attempted assassination of the Israeli ambassador to London by the ANO as the pretext for destroying the PLO. When Israeli Chief of Staff General Rafel Eitan was told by subordinates that the terrorists who shot Argov belonged to a group that loathed Arafat and Fatah, his intemperate response was as follows, "Abu Nidal? Abu Shmidal! They're all PLO!" The Israeli intervention may have destroyed the PLO's power in Lebanon, but it came at the cost of damaging the Jewish state's international reputation, and also led to the creation of a more dangerous enemy in the form of Hezbollah and the IR.[213]

Military operations against state sponsors are usually intended to coerce the target into ceasing its assistance to terrorist groups, or its instigation of attacks, but does coercion work? Defenders of retaliatory policy can point to the Clinton administration's response to an Iraqi plot to kill former President George H. W. Bush during a visit to Kuwait in April 1993. On June 26, the United States destroyed Iraqi intelligence headquarters with a volley of Tomahawk missiles. Saddam Hussein had been a persistent sponsor of terrorist organizations, notably the ANO and PLF, during the 1980s, but after the June 1993 missile strikes, he apparently curtailed his support for such groups. In contrast, Operation EL DORADO CANYON probably inspired Gaddafi to order the Lockerbie bombing of December 22, 1988, which killed 270 people, as an act of revenge.[214]

Escalation.

Reprisal raids can lead to interstate war, with the onus for such an outcome being shared by the state sponsor and the retaliating power. IDF attacks against the *Fedayeen* in Egypt during the early 1950s contributed to the worsening of tensions that preceded the Sinai war of October 1956. The Samu incident of November 1966, in which Israeli and Jordanian forces clashed following an IDF cross-border attack against Fatah, had a wider diplomatic impact, which led to the Six Day War from June 5-10, 1967.[215] A similar danger of escalation exists in Indo-Pakistani relations, particularly because of Pakistani sponsorship of groups like LET and HUM, who are involved in the Kashmir conflict and have launched attacks on India itself. Since May 1998, both India and Pakistan are declared nuclear powers, and a major terrorist incident on Indian soil has the potential to provoke a disastrous military confrontation. It was because of this that General Anthony Zinni, the then-commander in chief of U.S. Central Command (CENTCOM), telephoned Pakistani Chief of Staff General Jehangir Karamat on August 20, 1998, to inform him of the decision to launch Operation INFINITE REACH; U.S. officials feared that the Pakistanis would pick up Tomahawks bound for Afghan targets on their radar, assume that it was an Indian preemptive strike, and retaliate.[216]

The potential for war reemerged on December 13, 2001, when five terrorists from *Jaish e-Mohamed* (a Pakistani-backed group) launched a suicide bomb and gun attack on the Lok Sabha (the lower House of Parliament) in New Delhi. This attempt to slaughter Indian parliamentarians outraged public and political opinion and led to the massing of the Indian armed forces on the border with Pakistan, meeting a similar response from Islamabad. From December 2001 to October 2002, both countries were poised for confrontation, which was mitigated only by American diplomatic mediation.[217] The Mumbai attack of November 2008 also provoked popular demands within India for retaliation, although both the Indian and Pakistani governments managed to avoid a major crisis. Nonetheless, the possibility of a subcontinental Sarajevo—of a terrorist outrage provoking a cataclysmic Indo-Pakistani war—still exists. Indeed, it is likely that the Lok Sabha raid was intended by its instigators to provoke a major crisis, forcing Pakistan to send troops away from the FATA toward India, assisting the escape of al-Qaeda and Taliban fighters from the Coalition offensive in Afghanistan. The Mumbai attack may likewise have been intended by its LET instigators to cause a crisis that would see the removal of Pakistani Army units from the Afghan to the Indian border, thereby reducing the threat posed to the TTP and other allied groups.[218]

The Price of Intervention.

As demonstrated by the Israeli occupation of Southern Lebanon from 1982-2000 and NATO's current predicament in Afghanistan, a retaliatory or regime-change mission may lead to a prolonged occupation and the involvement of military forces in a debilitating and controversial struggle against insurgents. The Iraq war and current NATO operations in Afghanistan are also contributing to a growing sense among European and, to a lesser extent, U.S. public opinion that military intervention is in itself a source of insecurity, insofar as such operations alienate Islamic opinion, inciting Muslims in Western countries into committing atrocities such as the Madrid train station bombings of March 2004, and the July 7, 2005 (7/7) bombings in London.[219] While these perceptions may not be strictly accurate — the process of radicalization in Britain and other Western countries preceded the interventions in Afghanistan and Iraq — they are nonetheless prevalent. Such concerns, in conjunction with public disquiet over military losses, may compel the British and other allied governments into withdrawing their forces from Afghanistan, in much the same way as Israeli public opinion over the losses the IDF sustained in Southern Lebanon contributed to its withdrawal on May 24, 2000.[220]

PROBLEMS ARISING FROM MILITARY INVOLVEMENT IN COUNTERTERRORISM — THE DOMESTIC CONTEXT

Turning to the internal dimension of military intervention in counterterrorism, it is important to stress that democracy rests on the idea that governance is based on the consent of the majority and that any political disputes are resolved nonviolently. If changes to the political or socioeconomic order are required to address popular discontent, then these need to be affected incrementally, and by consensus on the process of reform, and not by either the application of violence from below (in the form of an insurrection) or above (in the form of an authoritarian coup). The ability to debate, to reason, and ultimately to persuade is a key feature of liberal democratic politics, as is a clear and understandable distaste for those who use intimidation and the application of force to achieve their objectives. The norms of democracy also stress the importance of the rule of law, that governments are bound by an implicit social contract with the governed, and that the worst crime a state's rulers can commit is to abuse the authority vested in them by the electoral process, and to turn governance by consent and responsibility into rule by fear.[221]

All of this means that the use of military means to fight domestic terrorism is fraught with political, practical, and ethical problems. No democratic politician should feel completely comfortable with the idea that the task of fighting terrorism should be entrusted to an organized body of men and women who are conditioned to the idea of using violence — albeit in a controlled and discriminate manner — to achieve set objectives, who adhere to principles of hierarchy and chain-of-command, and who are accustomed to the idea of identifying an enemy and planning and conducting a sequence of actions aimed at its destruction. The contradiction between democratic politics and the military ethos should be recognized. While it is dangerous to assume that the latter is superior to the former and also naïve to assume that democracy can survive against internal and external threats without any means of defense, the contradiction between the norms of the liberal democratic state and military realities is a key theme in this section. Students of civil-military relations in democracies recognize that the friction between the frock coats and the brass manifests itself in warfare against state-based adversaries.[222] The same is true of democracies beset by armed and lethally inclined internal enemies as well.

Resources.

A key question that governments need to ask is whether their armed forces actually have the assets and manpower needed to make a valid contribution to a counterterrorist campaign. A prime example is offered in the UK's case by the CCRF, the formation of which was announced in the MOD's *Strategic Defence Review: New Chapter* (2002). As of December 31, 2003, the CCRF officially consisted of 14 regional units 500-strong, nominally drawn from the Royal Naval Reserve, the Territorial Army and the Royal Auxiliary Air Force.[223] Yet the establishment of the CCRF failed to take account of the fact that that the British military's reservists were overwhelmingly committed to operations in Iraq and Afghanistan. Furthermore, the CCRF's exact relationship with the emergency services was unclear, particularly regarding the establishment of communications between the two, and few CCRF exercises have actually been conducted beyond the confines of London District. The CCRF was dismissed as a cosmetic exercise intended purely for public consumption. As one officer involved in its establishment complained, "[We] have a name and a role but no troops and no resources." Neither the Labour government nor the MOD gave any clear indication as to the CCRF's roles, or as to what assets it can rely on in responding to a major terrorist attack, and in this respect it is therefore fair to describe it as a "paper force."[224]

Boots on the Streets.

It is a rare and disturbing sight to see armed soldiers in full battle order, complete with webbing and ammunition, in public in a liberal democratic state. The sight of troops on the streets is instinctively unsettling. The average civilian can be forgiven for assuming that he or she may be shot dead for performing an innocuous action that may be interpreted by soldiers as a threat, while the more politically aware may wonder if the sudden presence of troops precedes a more sinister action, such as a coup d'etat. With a deterrence operation, one of the key problems for a state is how to prove a negative. No government can inform the media and the populace with true certainty that a decision to put soldiers on the streets definitely thwarted a terrorist attack, given the often imprecise nature of the intelligence involved. It will never be known for certain whether an al-Qaeda militant observed the deployment of the Grenadier Guards and Household Cavalry to Heathrow airport in February 2003 and decided to abort a planned attack. What is evident is that that this particular operation "freaked" several passengers out at the airport, particularly because the cavalry turned up with Scimitar reconnaissance vehicles that, to the inexpert eye, look like tanks. There was also widespread media skepticism about the alert, attributed as being an attempt by the Blair government to influence public opinion prior to the Anglo-American invasion of Iraq.[225]

The Heathrow alert of 2003 was treated by media critics as an example of New Labour spin. Similar operations nearly 30 years earlier aroused alarm rather than scorn. Following the implementation of Operation MARMION in January 1974, troops were deployed at the airport on at least three further occasions that year, in June, July, and September. These maneuvers occurred at a time of considerable economic and social upheaval, and while there were widespread rumors that the establishment was plotting to overthrow the Labour government. While right-wing commentators like former British Army General Walter Walker hysterically declared that increased trade union activism and industrial strikes were part of a Soviet-backed plot to destabilize Britain, many on the left believed that the armed forces were poised for a coup. The Heathrow deployments were therefore seen not as a response to a potential terrorist threat, but as a rehearsal for a military takeover.[226]

Fears of a military takeover in Britain during the 1970s were closely linked with the conflict in Northern Ireland. The *putsch* initiated by French commanders in Algeria in April 1961 set a precedent in which military frustration with an ongoing counterterrorist/COIN campaign might lead to resentment at the perceived obstructions imposed by a democratic order, and a growing sense among the officer corps that in order to win the war, the government needed to be overthrown. The British left's fear during the mid-1970s that the Army's frustrations with its inability to defeat PIRA, not to mention fragmentary evidence of military disaffection with the Wilson government, could lead to a coup therefore reflected the wider fears of civil strife and social collapse that were prevalent during that time.[227]

Chain of Command.

Operation BANNER, like other cases involving military intervention in counterterrorism, was also fraught with practical problems arising from the position of the Army within the decisionmaking hierarchy. It is an inevitable feature of bureaucratic politics that government departments and official agencies clash over departmental roles, procedures, and lines of administrative responsibility.[228] In Northern Ireland from 1969-72, the General Officer Commanding (GOC) was in charge of internal security, but the Chief Constable of the RUC possessed considerable autonomy. The GOC was also accountable not only to the British government in Westminster, answering to both the MOD and the Home Office, but also — before the imposition of direct rule by London on March 27, 1972 — to the devolved government at Stormont. Even after March 1972, the GOC of British forces took orders from the MOD and the Chief of the General Staff (CGS), but also the Northern Ireland Office (NIO).[229] This created several opportunities for bureaucratic infighting and departmental friction.

Such tensions were evident from August 1969, when British troops were sent to the province. While both the Labour and, after June 1970, the Conservative governments tried to focus on peacekeeping and preserving civil order, this agenda conflicted with Stormont's persistence in emphasizing the need to crush a Republican insurrection, rather than to deal even-handedly with both communities and to address the grievances of the Catholic community.[230] The first GOC, Lieutenant General Sir Ian Freeland, clashed constantly with RUC Chief Constable Arthur Young throughout 1969-70. Young had been appointed to reform the police—undermanned at 3,000 constables and compromised by its Unionist bias—but he angered Freeland by taking measures (notably disarming the force and reducing its role in public order control), which in the GOC's opinion increased the burden on the Army for maintaining internal security. Young, for his part, resented the fact that the RUC was often not consulted by its military counterparts and had no say in Army planning.[231]

The imposition of direct rule reduced the ability of the Unionist establishment to block reform, but it did not remove the tensions that existed between the Army and the RUC. The introduction of police primacy in 1976 was subsequently challenged by General Sir Timothy Creasey during his tenure as GOC. Creasey expressed frustration at what he considered to be feeble security force tactics, and publicly stated that the Army should "stop messing around and take out the terrorists." The Warrenpoint ambush on August 27, 1979, in which PIRA managed to kill 18 British soldiers in a skillfully planned double-bombing, only increased the GOC's fury. Although the newly-elected Conservative government overruled Creasey's requests to reassert Army control over the campaign against PIRA, his attitude was noteworthy. It is conceivable that in similar scenarios in the future other generals may react against what they consider to be unnecessary political and bureaucratic restraints on a counterterrorist campaign, particularly if they believe that military casualties are incurred as a consequence.[232]

The implementation of domestic counterterrorist measures in mainland Britain after 1972 was also hampered by interdepartmental wrangles. Police chiefs were initially uneasy with the prospects of calling in 22SAS's Pagoda troop to resolve an emergency, seeing the latter as a band of trigger-happy mavericks. The close attention 22SAS paid to liaison arrangements, in particular standardizing communications and arranging transport by air or land in the event of a crisis—in addition to the repeated visits paid by English, Scottish, and Welsh chief constables to the regiment's headquarters near Hereford—helped alleviate police concerns and did much to ensure close cooperation between 22SAS and the Metropolitan Police during Operation NIMROD.[233]

Preparations for maritime counterterrorist contingencies, with particular reference to the North Sea oilfields, during the mid-1970s were subject to a more intense bureaucratic quarrel, particularly regarding command and control measures. The Home Office backed Scottish police chiefs, who believed that they could be saddled with the responsibility for protecting oil platforms, despite their lack of the resources required. The MOD and the armed forces were, for their part, loath to commit military units to the defense of offshore installations against terrorist attack, particularly at a time when they faced both budget cuts and other significant commitments, notably regarding NATO and Operation BANNER.[234] The departments involved finally agreed in March 1977 to implement standard MACA principles; the Home Office would be responsible for handling any emergency, terrorist-related or otherwise, and the police authorities would only call for military assistance if they lacked the means to resolve it themselves. At the time of this writing, contingency preparations for a maritime terrorist attack off the UK coast have yet to be implemented, and indeed one SBS veteran expressed the view that offshore oil rigs are extremely difficult for terrorists to assault, not only because of their size but because of the character of their work force:

> I always felt it would take a particularly insane terrorist to actually try to capture a North Sea oil platform and then hold on to it. Many of the so-called roughnecks who work on them have military backgrounds. It would not be like taking over a cruise ship with a mostly elderly clientele and soft crew. If a terrorist turned his back for a second on one of these roughnecks, it is likely that his next experience would be a wrench crashing through his skull.[235]

During the 1970s, British civil servants and military personnel prepared themselves for a terrorist attack at sea, but in Mumbai in 2008 the Indians had to face a seaborne attack on a major city. The Indian authorities were criticized not only for the intelligence failure preceding the LET attacks, but also for the delay in calling in military reinforcements. It took the Indian Army 5.5 hours to respond, by which time the terrorists had claimed most of their victims. The attacks started at 9:20 p.m. on November 26, and local army units took to the streets at 2:50 a.m. the following morning. The arrival of India's elite counterterrorist unit, the National Security Guard (NSG), was delayed by nearly 10 hours; not only did the NSG have to fly from their base in Delhi, but it had no dedicated air force transport at its disposal. Since November 2008, the Indians have sought to enhance their capabilities for dealing with a similar attack, establishing joint patrol stations for the navy, police, and coastguard, as well as regional centers for the NSG. However, there are still considerable problems in interagency cooperation, not least the fact that the Indian Army, which provides officers to and training for the NSG, is loath to loan personnel to train and command this unit due to manpower shortages within its own officer corps.[236]

In Britain's case, COBRA worked well in handling the Iranian embassy siege in May 1980 mainly because Ministers and officials had time to deliberate over their actions. More recently, the Metropolitan Police's former chief of anti-terrorism, Andy Hayman, has expressed frustration with COBRA's sluggishness and the tendency of Ministers to interfere with what he regards as petty political considerations. Hayman's recommendations involve establishing a separate body for the police and other key agencies to prepare contingency plans for consideration by COBRA.[237] In this case, it would make sense to copy the standard Whitehall practice of shadowing Ministerial committees with official ones, particularly regarding advance preparation for and consideration of potential emergency scenarios.

The Intelligence Aspect.

One of the principal causes of interdepartmental animosity involves the means needed to gather information on a terrorist organization, its collation, and its dissemination across various agencies. Success depends on the security forces' ability to accurately identify terrorists, to obtain timely information about their operations, their objectives, and their overall strategy. Generating this information represents a considerable challenge, for, as Kitson noted, "the problem of defeating the enemy consists very largely of finding him." As noted in Section 2, vital sources of human intelligence (HUMINT) include undercover patrols, informants recruited from the civilian population, and agents (turned terrorists who are supplying information to the security forces). Both insurgents and terrorists understand the dangers posed by HUMINT sources; hence, their readiness to murder suspected agents and informants in order to intimidate the general populace into silence.[238]

One striking aspect concerning the historical record of both COIN and counterterrorism is the fact that—despite insurgent/terrorist intimidation, not to mention the profound racial, ethnic, cultural, and sectarian divides that can separate state authorities from the general population—security forces find it easy to recruit informants from the civil population, and to encourage insurgents and terrorists, often while the latter are in captivity, to change sides. This has been demonstrated not only in Northern Ireland, but also with the ability of Israel's *Shin Bet* to recruit Palestinian spies in the Occupied Territories.[239] The motives of informants and agents vary, they include: monetary gain; fear of imprisonment or as part of a bargain to keep relatives out of jail; petty resentments; or even a sense of remorse or disgust over atrocities committed by their comrades. Yet spies, narks, and touts have a disproportionate effect on a terrorist organization, as even the suspicion of treachery can be enough to turn members against each other, or to persuade a paranoid leadership to purge its ranks. Abu Nidal's destruction of his own organization during the late 1980s provides a graphic example of the paralyzing effect that the fear of betrayal can have on a group.[240]

However, if a state's intelligence and security services are unable to cooperate, any intelligence gathered is of limited value. Ronen Bergman describes the chaos involving competing Israeli services—*Mossad*, *Shin Bet*, and IDF intelligence—engaged with Hezbollah in Lebanon during the 1980s-1990s, quoting a *Shin Bet* officer who described the Israeli intelligence system's workings as a "drugged octopus." Inadequate cooperation was also evident in British colonial defeats such as Aden, where the inability of the regular Army and 22SAS to coordinate their intelligence-gathering activities led to at least one instance when undercover patrols mistook each other for terrorists and shot at each other.[241]

Operation BANNER involved four separate intelligence agencies: the Army's Intelligence Corps, the RUC's Special Branch (SB), MI5, and the Secret Intelligence Service (SIS) (the latter's involvement being justified by PIRA's external sources of assistance in Eire and the United States). The services involved sought information on PIRA, splinter Republican groups such as the Irish National Liberation Army (INLA), and also the Loyalist organizations. The information sought included background (political) intelligence on their objectives; operational (military) intelligence, notably contact or time-sensitive information on imminent terrorist attacks; and criminal intelligence intended to assist the prosecution of suspects— the latter being of greater importance once police primacy came into effect. The obvious question was, which agency was responsible for generating which type of HUMINT, and while the Army and MI5 apparently had a good working relationship, the Intelligence Corps and the RUC SB constantly clashed over the Army's clandestine patrolling and over agent running. The Army's involvement in plain-clothes activity during the early 1970s, with the Military Reaction Force and 14 Intelligence Company, was a product of the inadequacies and the demoralization of the SB at that time.[242]

The recovery of the RUC's intelligence-gathering

capacity from around 1975 onward led to a series of turf wars between the Army, derided by police officers as cowboys and amateurs, and the RUC—still regarded by military critics as being infiltrated by pro-Loyalist hard men. (One senior Army officer noted in the autumn of 1973 that at least 51 RUC officers were linked to "Protestant extremists.") The appointment in 1979 of the retired SIS chief, Sir Maurice Oldfield, as Security Coordinator appears to have helped delineate lines of communication and responsibility between agencies, while another important decision was the pooling of raw intelligence from the Army and police at the RUC's Castlereagh headquarters. Although interdepartmental friction persisted, it is clear that the combined British intelligence effort led to the penetration of PIRA and the recruitment of a network of agents throughout the 1980s and 1990s, the effects of which are discussed below.[243]

Two further points should be noted. The first is that terrorists and insurgents are fighting their own intelligence war as well, and the most effective organizations will penetrate the security services with their own double agents and recruit their own sources. This was as evident in Belfast in October 1972 when British Army undercover operations were betrayed by a Fred (a PIRA agent recruited by Army intelligence who decided to change sides a second time), as it was in Basra over 30 years later, where the Mahdi Army was able to breach British military security through its sources in the IPS and locally employed workers at Coalition bases.[244] The second concerns the ethical dimensions of HUMINT-gathering, which are explored in more detail later in this chapter.

Massacring the Innocents.

The key rationale for involving the armed forces in counterterrorism is to save lives. This motive is undermined in instances where a military intervention actually causes substantial casualties. In Russia, the increasing ruthlessness that Chechen separatists have shown during successive hostage takings — from the Budyonnovsk raid of June 16, 1995, in which the Chechens raided this Southern Russian city, taking over a hospital in the process; to the Beslan school siege of September 1-3, 2004 — have presented the Russian authorities with a series of complex crises. In each case the civilian death toll has been high; 129 civilians were killed in Budyonnovsk, at least 28 in the Pervomayskoye crisis in Dagestan (January 12-18, 1996), 130 in the *Nord-Ost* theatre siege (October 23, 2002), and a minimum of 338 (including 156 schoolchildren) at Beslan, North Ossetia.[245] Yet these losses have not simply been due to Chechen brutality, but also to a combination of ruthlessness and official incompetence on the part of the Russian government and its security forces — not just the army, but the Federal Security Service (FSB) and the MVD.

At Budyonnovsk and Pervomayskoye, surviving hostages testified that many of the dead were caused by indiscriminate shooting on the part of the security forces. In the latter case, the Russians bombarded a village occupied by Chechen separatists and their Dagestani hostages with tanks and multiple rocket launchers. The Chechens were not only able to repel repeated attacks by MVD troops, but the bulk of them were able to break through the Russian cordon and escape back into Chechnya.[246] All but two of the hostages who died during the *Nord-Ost* tragedy were killed by a supposedly nonlethal incapacitating gas that FSB *spetsnaz* troops pumped into the theatre; the Russian authorities even neglected to inform medical personnel treating casualties as to the nature of the agent they used, thereby hampering their ability to treat them. As for Beslan, while Moscow insisted that Russian soldiers only stormed the school after the terrorists started to detonate bombs, a *Duma* (parliamentary) commission reported that *spetsnaz* soldiers may have started the final firefight in which so many hostages died. While scholars need to treat competing claims about these incidents cautiously, the manner with which the Russian state has dealt with hostage crises reflects the over-militarized and repressive manner in which both the Yelstin and Putin governments fought their wars against Chechen separatists.[247]

The consequences of a bloody counterterrorist operation can also be seen in the aftermath of Operation BLUE STAR in India (June 3-6, 1984). The Golden Temple at Amritsar, the most sacred shrine of the Sikh faith, had been taken over and fortified by armed separatists fighting for an independent Kalistan. On June 3, the Indian Prime Minister Indira Gandhi ordered the army to storm the temple, and after 3 days of fighting (which involved a total of 70,000 troops, backed by tanks and armored vehicles) the Indian military recaptured the shrine and killed several hundred militants, including their leader, Jarnail Singh Bhindranwale. Unfortunately, Operation BLUE STAR led to the death of at least 1,000 people, many of them pilgrims. While the majority of Sikhs were enraged that separatists had defiled the Golden Temple, the Indian Army's response outraged opinion in the Punjab, and was seen as a gross act of mass murder and sacrilege. Operation BLUE STAR therefore inflamed the Punjabi insurgency, and the most immediate consequence was Gandhi's assassination by two of her bodyguards, both Sikhs, on October 31, 1984.[248]

The implications of killing unarmed civilians were also evident, albeit on a smaller scale, in Northern Ireland in the early 1970s. Troops involved in MACP missions are likely to become involved in violent contingencies short of outright terrorism, such as a public order incident (a riot) involving elements of the local population. In Belfast and Londonderry, the ability of British soldiers to contain rioters was tested to the limit. The British Army's public order training emphasizes the controlled use of force to deescalate a riot, but in practice the stress of dealing not only with stone-throwers, but also petrol bombers and snipers meant that soldiers could (and did) shoot unarmed people, thereby inflaming Catholic hostility toward the military even further.[249] The disastrous end to a Northern Ireland Civil Rights Association march in Londonderry on Bloody Sunday (January 30, 1972) was the most extreme example. Troops from Support Company, 1st Battalion Parachute Regiment (1PARA), responded to what they considered to be incoming fire by shooting into a crowd of demonstrators, killing 13 of them. The result was an international scandal that was a propaganda coup for PIRA. Much of the blame for Bloody Sunday has been placed on the aggressive ethos of the paratroopers, who had collectively alienated the Catholic population and had even caused distaste and concern among other Army units. When 1PARA deployed in Londonderry in mid-January 1972, a soldier from another battalion who saw them arrive exclaimed, "Christ, we're here to stop protesters, not kill them!"[250] The paras vigorously dispute claims that they were trigger-happy, and the Saville inquiry into the shootings has shown Republican gun-men did actually shoot at the soldiers prior to the kill-ings. However, even with the advantage of hindsight, it is hard to dispute Thomas Hennessey's verdict on Bloody Sunday:

> The best that can be said is that, in an alien environ-ment the paratroopers who opened fire saw threats from all quarters once they had been fired upon: rocks became nail bombs, rifles were seen peering out from barricades when in fact there were none. The alterna-tive is that this was murder. Somewhere between the two is probably the truth.[251]

Minimum Force/Hearts and Minds.

Bloody Sunday illustrates a serious problem in MACP, which is that the deployment of troops can antagonize the civilian population, particularly if they are perceived by a section of the populace as being brutal and repressive, as was the case in Northern Ire-land. The fact is, as a former British Army officer, Col-onel Michael Dewar noted, "No army, however well it conducts itself, is suitable for police work."[252] Neither the problem of applying minimum force (minimum by whose standards?) nor the issues posed by applying lethal force in self-defense (When is it justified? What happens if a soldier misjudges a situation and shoots an innocent civilian?) should be regarded as unique to Operation BANNER. They have also been shown in the Kashmir insurgency from 1989 onward, with criti-cisms of the conduct of the Indian Army and paramili-tary troops from the BSF toward Kashmiri civilians. One Indian Army Brigadier offered the following ex-planation in an interview in April 1995, which could be uttered by almost any military commander faced with an elusive enemy who hides amongst the civilian population and who only exposes himself or herself prior to an attack:

> The aim of the soldier is to kill or capture; win or lose he must apply maximum force because of military considerations. But in Kashmir overnight he has to do a flip-flop. There is no enemy with whom he can identify. It is his own people who have taken up arms against him. Therefore, although you can win militarily you can lose the war.[253]

A similar problem appears to have manifested itself in Northwest Pakistan, judging by press reports of extrajudicial killings of TTP suspects following the recapture of the Swat Valley in February 2009, which are attributed to (and denied by) the Pakistani Army.[254]

The recruitment of local military forces can contribute to tensions between the armed forces and the civilian population, particularly if, in cases where terrorism exists alongside profound ethnic, racial, or sectarian differences, these are seen to be representative of one particular community. In 1970 the British established the Ulster Defence Regiment (UDR) as a territorial force to supplement Army operations. The UDR became particularly important from the mid-1970s, when the British government sought to cut troop numbers in Northern Ireland due to the fact that the Army was overstretched meeting its NATO commitments.[255]

The problem was that the UDR was overwhelmingly Protestant in character; by 1985, out of 6,500 soldiers, only 175 were Catholics, in spite of British efforts to recruit a nonsectarian force. This was partly due to the fact that PIRA threatened to murder potential and actual Catholic recruits, but there was also a widespread feeling within the Catholic community that the UDR was institutionally linked to the Loyalist movement. The involvement of some of its soldiers in Loyalist atrocities, shown by the conviction of 16 of its number for murder between 1970 and 1989, did little to improve the UDR's reputation. Its defenders may describe this as the behavior of a minority within its ranks, but the fact remains that the UDR was not seen by Catholics as an impartial force. As one councilor of the moderate Nationalist SDLP stated, "[no] one [in the Catholic community] considers the UDR to be part of the British Army . . . . They are seen as a Loyalist militia. They behave, in many cases, like a Loyalist militia." UDR veterans would no doubt view this statement as a slur on their regimental honor, but it is clear that this force's reputation was as much a disincentive for Catholics to join as threats from PIRA. Despite the British government's efforts to create a territorial force representative of both communities, the UDR was seen by many Catholics as a successor to the disbanded B Specials.[256]

Accountability.

In certain cases, military intelligence and Special Forces units involved in counterterrorism have faced accusations that they have become involved in so-called "black operations." These include assassinations and false flag attacks (atrocities committed by military or security force personnel, which are then blamed on terrorists), and they reflect the fear that the soldiers concerned are beyond oversight or control by civilian authorities. In Italy during the late 1960s, when the BR first emerged, left-wing critics blamed officers from the military intelligence service (SID) for inciting neo-Fascist terrorist outrages. The supposed objective of this strategy of tension was to frame the extreme left for the ensuing bloodshed, thereby creating the conditions for a military coup. It is difficult to determine to what degree these accusations were true, or whether they reflect the enduring appeal of *dietrologia* (behind-ology), the term used to describe the Italian penchant for conspiracy theories.[257]

Britain had its own version of the SID scandal with the activities of the Military Reaction Force (MRF) in Northern Ireland (1971-72). This plain-clothes British Army unit had been set up as a clandestine intelligence-gathering team, but its members became involved in at least five incidents in which civilians were shot. PIRA claimed that the MRF were *agents provocateurs* working to inflame sectarian tensions, so that the British state could claim that it was trying to stop a civil war between Catholics and Protestants. A contrasting view is offered by the Northern Irish journalist Martin Dillon, who described British military intelligence operations during the early 1970s as a product of amateurism and poor training. The Army hierarchy's dissatisfaction with the MRF, and its determination to control clandestine activity and prevent individual battalions from engaging in piratical ventures, led to the formation of 14 Intelligence Company in January 1973; this was an established unit operating under the command of the GOC's deputy, the Commander Land Forces, Northern Ireland.[258] Nonetheless, Republican propaganda and critics continued to emphasize the nefarious character of British military undercover activity, although the general tendency (notably after 22SAS was deployed to Armagh in January 1976) was to attribute all clandestine operations to the "Special Assassination Squads."[259]

Turkey offers a clear example where a fragile democratic state has found it difficult to control its armed forces. In 1952, the Turkish Army formed a Special Warfare Group (OHD) as a stay-behind force, a skeleton resistance group to be activated in the event of a Soviet invasion. However, there is evidence to suggest that the OHD directed organized criminal gangs and the far-right Grey Wolves in false flag attacks attributed to leftist terrorists during the 1970s-1980s. In Kurdistan during the 1980s-1990s a plain-clothes *jandarma* intelligence unit (JITEM) used former PKK insurgents to assassinate former comrades, and also allegedly became involved in drug smuggling. Both the OHD and JITEM were linked to what Turks call the *derin devlet* (deep state), and are also connected with the current scandal involving an apparent plot by a secret organization of army and *jandarma* officers (known as *Ergenekon*) to overthrow the *Adelet ve Kalkinma Partish* (AKP) government.[260]

Clandestine military intelligence activity in counterterrorism will almost inevitably arouse wild rumors, conspiracy-theorizing, black propaganda, and genuine concerns about accountability. The likelihood that a state's armed and security forces are involved in unsavory and destabilizing actions under the guise of fighting terrorism cannot always be discounted, particularly in cases where the state's democratic foundations are weak. Yet, the array of conspiracy theories that 9/11 and 7/7 were false flag attacks staged by the U.S. and British governments, respectively, show that *dietrologia* and fears of the *derin devlet* are not exclusively Italian or Turkish characteristics.[261] Furthermore, insurgent and terrorist groups may deliberately use false flag claims to absolve themselves of responsibility for civilian attacks; hence, the claim by the TTP and other Islamist militants that U.S. contractors from Xe Services are responsible for the bomb attacks that have struck Peshawar, Karachi, Rawalpindi, and other Pakistani cities in recent months.[262]

Jus in bello.

LOAC stresses that if military actions are to be legitimate in war (*in bello*), they must be proportionate and discriminate, and since 1977 the Geneva Conventions on the treatment of prisoners of war and civilians are also explicitly applicable to internal as well as external conflicts.[263] The difficulties of applying these principles in practice can be seen in the controversies surrounding five aspects where the military have either become or are potentially involved in counterterrorism: the interception of hijacked aircraft, the legal status of terrorists suspects in custody, hostage rescue, preemptive intervention and targeted killing, and agent running.

Interception of hijacked aircraft. Since 9/11, the prospects of a similar attack—in which suicide hijackers take over a passenger plane and crash it into a city, a nuclear power plant, or another high-value target—have led some governments to prepare contingency plans to shoot down hijacked aircraft. Examples include the establishment of the RAF's QRA squadron and also the revised orders given to the Federal Aviation Authority and North American Air Defense Command (NORAD) after 9/11. On the morning of the al-Qaeda attacks on New York and Washington, DC, NORAD had only four fighters from the Air National Guard at its disposal to protect the entire U.S. Eastern seaboard. Prior to 9/11, NORAD contingency planning did not anticipate a scenario in which a domestic airliner would be taken over and turned into a suicide craft. Since September 2001, NORAD operates at a higher state of readiness, and in the 2 years that followed 9/11, the U.S. and Canadian air forces scrambled jets on 1,500 occasions, mainly in response to false alarms, such as a temporary loss of contact with a passenger jet.[264]

Yet the prospects of another 9/11-style attack present democratic states with an appalling dilemma: Governments can either order fighter pilots to intercept and destroy hijacked planes, complete with passengers and crew, in mid-air, or accept the inevitable loss of civilian life when the aircraft is either driven into its target or runs out of fuel and crashes.[265] This scenario also raises two further potentially disturbing possibilities. The first is that an airliner can be shot down if its pilot loses contact with air traffic control, and nervous officials assume that the plane has been hijacked. The second is that in the aftermath of a shoot-down, members of the terrorist group responsible for the initial hijacking can issue a statement denying that they intended to use the plane for a suicide attack, claiming that they intended to land the aircraft and issue demands. They then are able to accuse the responsible government of mass murder.

Legal status of terrorist suspects. As noted above, intelligence is of crucial importance in counterterrorism, and one means of gaining this is the interrogation of suspects in custody. Even if one disregards obvious extremes, such as the French in Algeria, the issue of how detainees are treated in military custody is a contentious one. The British Army enraged the Catholic community and the Irish government when it introduced internment without trial for Republican terrorist suspects on August 9, 1971. Further outrage was caused

109

by public disclosure of the so-called "deep interrogation" or CALABA methods—hooding, sleep deprivation, stress positions—used on some detainees. An official government inquiry reported, much to the fury of the then-Prime Minister Edward Heath, that the treatment associated with deep interrogation constituted physical ill-treatment. What was significant was that these interrogation methods had been used by the Army in previous British COIN campaigns, although they had been modified after a scandal involving detainee abuse in Aden. The furor surrounding deep interrogation led to the abandonment of these coercive methods, although this did not prevent further accusations of ill-treatment both by *Sinn Fein* and domestic critics in the UK. Furthermore, although internment had negative political consequences, its actual implementation, which involved 1,981 detainees between 1971 and 1975, provided the Army and the RUC with crucial intelligence on PIRA and its principal Republican rival, the Official IRA. Nonetheless, the fact that only 107 suspected Loyalists were detained under internment contributed to the sense of persecution and injustice that many in the Catholic community felt. The fact that the British authorities treated Loyalist violence as, to quote Paul Dixon, "a symptom of [PIRA's] campaign," was a strategic blunder; internment may have been easier for Catholics to accept if Protestant extremists were seen to be treated to the same process as suspected Republican terrorists.[266]

The current War on Terror also highlights the problems involved in detaining terrorist suspects. The Bush administration's decision to authorize the U.S. military to use similar methods on detainees in Guantanamo Bay on the grounds that al-Qaeda and Taliban captives are not eligible to prisoner of war status under the terms of the Geneva Convention not only had a negative effect on international opinion, but it also created a legal quagmire for the U.S. Government. Although the U.S. military is responsible for guarding the detainees at Guantanamo Bay, Cuba, this controversy is not actually of its making. During the summer of 2003, representatives of the Judge Advocate General's Corps (JAG) from the Army, Navy, Marine Corps, and Air Force vigorously protested against aggressive counter-resistance techniques on moral grounds, due to concerns about their country's reputation and fears that it would set a precedent for the maltreatment of U.S. service personnel held prisoner in future conflicts. The implications of Guantanamo Bay would be best debated in a separate paper, but the key concerns here are not only those outlined by the JAG, but the fact that coercive techniques such as water-boarding tarnish the trials of individuals like Khalid Sheikh Mohamed, the architect of the 9/11 attacks.[267] It also appears as though such guidance on counter-resistance techniques has led to military abuses akin to the Abu Ghraib scandal of 2003, such as the maltreatment of suspected Taliban and al-Qaeda detainees in Bagram and other U.S. military bases in Afghanistan, and even some deaths in custody.[268]

Hostage rescue. Traditional hostage-rescue missions can also present ethical problems, particularly related to the use of minimum force. With Operation NIMROD it is clear that then-Prime Minister Margaret Thatcher wanted to take a tough line with the Ahvaz hostage takers to ensure that the British government was not perceived as being soft in the face of terrorist threats. However, during Operation NIMROD, at least two of the gunmen shot dead are supposed to have laid down their arms in an attempt to surrender.

One SAS veteran subsequently stated that he and his comrades received the following orders prior to the assault:

> The message was that we had to resolve the situation and there was to be no chance of failure, and that the hostages absolutely had to be protected. The Prime Minister did not want an ongoing problem beyond the embassy—which we took to mean that they didn't want anybody coming out alive. No surviving terrorists.[269]

Other ex-SAS soldiers involved cannot confirm that these orders were given, and the following points need to be considered before judging whether there was a policy to summarily execute the hostage takers. First, the Ahvaz gunmen had already murdered one of the Iranian embassy staff, and during the rescue mission they tried to kill more hostages. Second, one of the lessons 22SAS took from the Munich massacre was that any assault had to be conducted with such speed and aggression that the terrorists would be overwhelmed before they could either retaliate or start executing their captives, and this calculation shaped the planning and implementation of Operation NIMROD. Third, prior to this mission 22SAS had lost one of their officers, Captain Herbert Westmacott, at the beginning of a siege involving PIRA gunmen in Belfast. Westmacott's death would have complemented the lessons learnt from repeated exercises, which was that until the Iranian Embassy was successfully secured, any hesitation in using lethal force against the terrorists could lead to the deaths of SAS personnel or hostages.[270]

Premptive intervention and targeted killing. The outcome of the Iranian embassy siege was less controversial than cases of preemptive intervention involving the Army and the RUC in Northern Ireland. The
Loughgall ambush was regarded by military officials
as a clean operation because the eight PIRA volunteers killed were armed and clearly involved in an imminent attack on an RUC station. An alternate view
stresses that the terrorists could have been intercepted
and arrested en route to Loughgall, and that the ambush also caused the unnecessary death of one civilian who was shot dead by mistake by the SAS. With
this in mind, it appears as though the British Army
subsequently took greater pains to try to capture
armed terrorists alive. This was demonstrated by the
arrest of the South Armagh sniper, Michael Caraher,
and his three accomplices by 22SAS in April 1997.[271]
There were also more controversial cases in which innocent civilians were killed by British Special Forces
soldiers, and even one case in which "ordinary decent
criminals" ended up in the firing line, namely the three
bank robbers killed in West Belfast by 14 Intelligence
Company on January 13, 1990.[272]

The most contentious shooting remains that which
occurred at the end of Operation FLAVIUS in Gibraltar on March 6, 1988, when three PIRA terrorists —
Mairead Farrell, Danny McCann, and Sean Savage —
were shot dead by 22SAS. Contrary to initial British
government statements, none of the three were armed,
and reports that they had smuggled a car bomb onto
the peninsula were also incorrect. This device was
supposed to be intended for a military parade, but the
explosives and vehicle were still in Spain at the time
the three were intercepted and killed. The Gibraltar
shootings were cited by media critics as examples

of a shoot-to-kill policy, in which both in Northern Ireland and overseas British forces sought to summarily execute suspects who could theoretically be apprehended. In response, Army sources refer to the hazards of trying to arrest terrorist suspects who are potentially armed—as one intelligence officer noted, PIRA gunmen did not "shoot to tickle"—and the danger that a soldier who hesitated in using force in self-defense could endanger himself or his comrades. It is also worth noting that Gibraltar had a knock-on effect. Mourners at Farrell, McCann, and Savage's funerals on March 16 were subjected to a grenade and gun attack by Michael Stone, a Loyalist terrorist. When one of Stone's victims was being buried three days later, a mob lynched two British Army corporals in civilian dress. Deaths may have been prevented in Gibraltar, but not in Northern Ireland.[273]

As Peter Taylor notes, the British Army and security forces in Northern Ireland were generally "not in the business of going into republican or loyalist areas and just taking terrorists out." In Israel's case, however, there is a declared policy of targeted killing directed against Palestinian terrorists. For critics like the Israeli NGO B'Tselem, the IDF's policy is immoral and illegal. B'Tselem highlights cases where innocent Palestinians have been shot dead, and its activists also argue that *Mista-aravim* soldiers are not entitled to claim shootings in self-defense, because they have deliberately placed themselves in a situation where they are obliged to kill. B'Tselem estimates that between 2000 and 2008, 202 Palestinians were subjected to targeted killings by the *Mista-aravim*, uniformed military personnel, or in air strikes, with an additional 121 bystanders being killed as a consequence.[274]

Aside from the ethical debate, it is also far from clear whether such strikes actually significantly disrupt Hamas, PIJ, and other Palestinian militant groups. The principal conclusions of a statistical analysis conducted by Mohammed Hafez and Joseph Hatfield in 2005-06 was that "targeted assassinations have no significant impact on the rates of Palestinian violence, even when time lags associated with possible retaliations are taken into account," and that the progressive decline in Palestinian suicide bombings and other attacks from 2002 could be attributable to other factors (such as the cease-fire between Fatah and Israel, and the construction of a separation wall between Israel and the West Bank). Cronin also argues that targeted killings have actually had more of an effect on inflaming Palestinian anger at Israel than civilian deaths. A prime example was the killing of Yahya Ayyash, a Hamas bomb maker nicknamed "The Engineer," by a booby-trapped mobile phone on January 5, 1996. Ayyash's death led to a fresh wave of suicide attacks against Israeli citizens in the following 2 months. While the IDF has scored several tactical successes in eliminating key personnel in Hamas, PIJ and other terrorist organizations, these have done nothing to resolve Israel's essential problem, which is the fierce hatred that many Palestinians feel toward the Jewish state, and their desire to destroy it.[275]

Agent running. Shooting terrorists causes enough trouble for a democratic government; recruiting them as agents poses further problems. The best source of HUMINT on the hierarchy, organization, personnel, and strategy of a terrorist group often comes from any of its members who can be recruited as spies. In Northern Ireland, Army intelligence, the RUC SB and MI5 were able to progressively paralyze PIRA through a combination of agent recruitment and clandestine surveillance. By 1992, five out of six of its planned attacks were being thwarted by the security forces. One senior Provisional, Brendan Hughes, confirms that the latter were able to "bring [PIRA] to a standstill," stating that "they were able to effectively stop the IRA and contain it" by the time its leadership declared their ceasefire on July 19, 1997.[276] Yet the operations of the FRU in Northern Ireland from 1980 onward highlight the ethical dangers involved in such activity. For agents to remain useful, they have to divert suspicion from themselves, and for a terrorist source this means remaining active and also continuing to perpetrate criminal acts. This was demonstrated by the FRU's recruitment of PIRA members, which allegedly included Alfredo Scappaticci, the head of the organization's internal security unit, nicknamed the "Nutting Squad" because it tortured and summarily executed suspected touts. If Scappaticci was an FRU agent, then it is more than likely that he murdered people, including other agents allegedly sacrificed by their security forces handlers, while working for the British Army.[277]

Even more disturbing is the case of Brian Nelson, a Loyalist paramilitary charged in 1990 with the murder of Belfast lawyer Patrick Finucane. Nelson was also an FRU agent, and his recruitment was regarded by the Catholic community as evidence of collusion; that Loyalist terrorists were used by the British state for the extrajudicial killing of Republicans and troublesome individuals like Finucane in a dirty war. The issue of agent recruitment therefore poses a series of moral dilemmas. To what extent does the recruitment of terrorists as government spies actually save lives by preventing bloody attacks? Does this justify the losses that are incurred by keeping such agents active? For example, the apparent guidance given to Nelson was to direct his comrades' attacks against known Republican rivals, rather than Catholic civilians, and to fake tip-offs to protect genuine agents — such as the one in which the FRU was alleged to have diverted the Loyalists away from Scappaticci to another Republican of Italian descent, Franscesco Notarantonio, who was assassinated in October 1987. Furthermore, in a contemporary environment where al-Qaeda and its affiliates plan and commit atrocities far bloodier than those committed by PIRA and its Loyalist foes, how can the military and security services of any democratic state contemplate the long-term recruitment and cultivation of intelligence sources within jihadi groups?[278]

Creeping Authoritarianism.

Historical experience has shown that a counterterrorist campaign has provided the pretext for military commanders, or an unscrupulous civilian leadership, to subvert the democratic order and establish dictatorial rule. A prime example is that of Uruguay during the early 1970s; the army's intervention decisively defeated the Tupamaros, but it also led to the military-sponsored dictatorship declared by President Juan Maria Bordaberry in June 1973.[279] While Alberto Fujimori was President of Peru from 1990-2000, he oversaw the military and police campaign that curtailed *Sendero Luminoso*'s threat to the state, but he also established a corrupt authoritarian regime with the *auto-golpe* of April 5, 1992.[280]

The most notorious example of this process during the latter half of the 20th century is that of Argentina during the late 1970s. Left-wing terrorist violence in that country was exceeded by the savagery of the dirty war waged by the armed force's *junta* that seized power on March 24, 1976. The era of military rule, 1976-83, was characterized by a period of lawlessness and barbarity in which the state showed a complete disregard for the distinction between terrorism and legitimate political dissent. While leftist groups such as the *Montoneros* and the *Ejército Revolucionario del Pueblo* were responsible for more than 3,000 kidnappings and murders between 1976 and 1979, the military *junta* is estimated to have killed at least 15,000 people, with a minimum of 9,000 "disappeared" between 1976 and 1983. General Jorge Videla, Argentina's dictator until March 29, 1981, epitomized the regime's attitude when describing a terrorist as "not just someone with a gun or a bomb, but also someone who spreads ideas that are contrary to Western and Christian civilization." The military's torturers and executioners acted on this guidance. In their campaign against terrorism, they rejected such anti-Christian vices as mercy and compassion, not to mention "subversive concepts alien to" Western civilization such as *habeas corpus* and due process before the law.[281]

There is also a clear danger that states that militarize the struggle against terrorism and succumb to authoritarianism may well destabilize themselves. This has become evident with the war against Chechen separatism that the Russians have waged since September 1999. Although the Russian military and MVD's anti-terrorist mission in Chechnya was declared over in April 2009, the Russian Federation's security forces have stirred up further instability in the North Caucasus as a consequence of their crackdown on indigenous Islam.[282] The October 13, 2005, attack by Islamist gunmen on Nalchik, the capital of the Republic of Karbadino-Balkar, and ongoing violence in

Ingushetia and Dagestan, the North Caucasian republics neighboring Chechnya, suggest that Moscow's resort to armed force against indigenous separatists on Russia's Southern frontier has actually incited more armed opposition to Federal rule. Recent years have not only shown an increase in the rate of lethal terrorist attacks across the North Caucasus (40 in 2006, 114 in 2007, 268 in 2008, and over 500 in 2009), but also the coalescence of jihadist groups across Ingushetia, Chechnya, Dagestan, and other neighboring republics. The implications for the Russian Federation's stability remain to be seen.[283]

A similar conclusion can be drawn following the formal end of Colombo's war with the LTTE in late-May 2009. The Tamil Tigers were justly reviled for their use of suicide bombing, for conscripting child soldiers, and also for using Tamil civilians as human shields in the face of the Sri Lankan Army's offensive, thereby contributing to the thousands of casualties suffered at the climax of the conflict. Former LTTE leader, Vellupilai Prabhakaran, also had a Stalinist attitude toward his ethnic kin manifested by his willingness to murder rival Tamil leaders who challenged his absolute authority over his people. Yet, the barbarity of the LTTE does not justify the blatant chauvinism of the Sinhalese-dominated government, or the appalling conditions experienced by Tamil civilians in Army-run refugee camps in the war's aftermath.[284] An additional disturbing trend includes the erosion of Sri Lanka's democratic system. Journalists, medics and other civil society figures are subjected to state sanctioned intimidation when examining the less savory aspects of the LTTE's defeat—notably the numbers of civilians killed in the last phases of the war, or the treatment of internally displaced Tamils in army-run refugee camps. Former Chief of the Defence Staff General Sarath Fonseka, widely credited with victory over the LTTE, was also imprisoned after standing in the February 2010 Presidential election against the incumbent, Mahinda Rajapaksa, and was charged with unspecified military offences.[285] The suppression of legitimate opposition by President Rajapaksa, officially sanctioned Sinhalese chauvinism, and enduring Tamil grievances of deprivation and disenfranchisement could all contribute to the resumption of communal and ethnic violence in the foreseeable future.

CONCLUSIONS

The underlying theme of this paper is that while the use of military means to fight terrorist organizations can have clear drawbacks and unwelcome consequences, this does not necessarily mean that a democratic state should eschew the use of the armed forces as part of an overall counterterrorism policy. The requirement to call in the military depends on a variety of factors: whether the terrorist threat is domestic or international; whether the civilian authorities and police/gendarmerie services can cope with the problem; whether positive or negative historical experiences, notably residual memories of Nazism and Fascism in post-war Germany and Italy, influence the ability of a government to request military support; and whether public opinion supports the use of such means. It is also evident that international support is crucial, whether this is with reference to the (admittedly wavering) levels of support for Operation ENDURING FREEDOM in the United States and allied countries, or the effect that Predator strikes in Pakistan are having on relations between Washington, DC, and Islamabad.

There may indeed be specific situations—such as MACA/MACP, hostage rescue, deterrence, training allied forces, and even a response to a Mumbai-style attack—where the military alone has the means to contain the threat terrorism poses to society, or to resolve a specific crisis. The problem with the post-9/11 War on Terror is not the fact that the United States and its allies have employed their armed forces against al-Qaeda and affiliated groups; it is the fact that the militarization of counterterrorism has taken place in a political and strategic vacuum. In the case of the Bush administration, the conduct of the War on Terror/ Long War was governed more by party-political posturing and electoral calculations than any long-term thinking.[286]

The change in administrations in Washington in January 2009 appears to have encouraged a systematic reevaluation of U.S. counterterrorist and national security policy. Indeed, even before President Obama took office, Secretary of Defense Robert Gates publicly stated that:

> What is dubbed the War on Terror is, in grim reality, a prolonged, worldwide irregular campaign—a struggle between the forces of violent extremism and moderation. In the long-term effort against terrorist networks and other extremists, **we know that direct military force will continue to have a role.** But we also understand that over the long term we cannot kill or capture our way to victory. Where possible, **kinetic operations should be subordinate to measures to promote better governance, economic programs to spur development, and efforts to address the grievances amongst the discontented from which the terrorists recruit.** It will take the patient accumulation of quiet successes over a long time to discredit and defeat extremist movements and their ideology.[287]

In Britain's case, the Labour government did bequeath to the current coalition a declared strategy in the form of CONTEST, but neither Tony Blair nor Gordon Brown paid any significant attention to the consideration of how resources should be allocated to fulfill the **prevent, pursue, protect,** and **prepare** aspects of CONTEST—the fiasco over the CCRF being a case in point. As far as military means were concerned, the British armed forces were expected to fulfill their counterterrorist missions overseas—most notably in Afghanistan—and domestically, despite successive cuts which left the defense budget at 2.2 percent of national income.[288] The current coalition administration is committed to sharp reductions in government expenditure, and it is inevitable that the SDSR will lead to further cuts for the MOD. It remains to be seen whether David Cameron's government will deliver the integrated National Security Strategy its Ministers have promised, and whether this will give the UK's armed forces the resources and manpower required to fulfill all its tasks, including those related to counterterrorism.[289]

Both the U.S. and British examples demonstrate that democratic governments dealing with a terrorist threat need to return to that much-overused but little understood term, namely **strategy**. In an issue as important as national security, strategy is about deciding what means should be employed to achieve specific goals. In counterterrorism, these means include economic power; diplomatic means; the legal resources of a state, police, and judiciary; the use of intelligence gained by a state's security and foreign espionage services; and the employment of military power. In this respect, the government's task is to decide which means are best used to resolve specific problems arising from terrorism, whether domestic or international.[290]

Yet, to begin this process of deliberation, a government needs to formulate an overall objective, an **end** to which **means** are to be applied. The objective of any liberal democracy involved in any conflict against terrorism should be the preservation of constitutional order and the basic tenets of a liberal state and society; a government's accountability to the elected representatives of the people; the preservation of governance by law and not by force, etc.; but also the protection of the security and the rights of its citizens, foremost among them **the right to life**. The latter applies not only to minimizing the ability of terrorists to kill and maim members of the general public, but also to ensuring that civilians are not exposed to excessive violence by the state and its agencies, as experienced by Argentina in the 1970s, and is evident in Russia and Sri Lanka today. Nearly 2 decades ago, Roland Crelinstein and Alex Schmid observed that "when agents of the state begin consistently to shoot suspects without bothering to arrest them, or to mistreat them during interrogation in order to force confessions, then the state has moved far along the road to a regime of terror."[291] That observation of the potential consequences of counterterrorism without an overarching strategic and political context has not lost its relevance.

The identification of a strategic objective provides a focus for a government involved in any form of conflict against an armed foe, whether state or nonstate in character. However, in deciding which means are needed to achieve overall strategic goals, and how these should be related to each other, decisionmakers face a challenge familiar to that which a school pupil encounters when presented with a quadratic equation in a math class. The student has the hard task of translating an algebraic formula into arithmetic; the policymaking elite involved in counterterrorism has to resolve a series of dilemmas related to specific decisions. Western countries involved in the conflict in Afghanistan have to contend with the fact that intervention in that country is exploited by radical Islamist ideologues to radicalize would-be militants, on the grounds that a jihad needs to be waged to defend Islam. Yet, any decision to disengage militarily from Afghanistan also runs the risk of encouraging al-Qaeda and its affiliates at their victory, inspiring more support for their cause and reenergizing their efforts. Likewise, UAV strikes against al-Qaeda militants in Northwest Pakistan and Yemen might have a discernible effect in weakening their network, but it might also anger public opinion in both countries, and cause resentment among friendly governments over the infringement of their sovereignty. In a domestic context, the democratic state faces the problem familiar from Northern Ireland in the 1970s to Western Europe today, that a government's measures to contain terrorist violence and to crack down on specific groups can actually alienate a section of the population and foster a perception of persecution and discrimination, thereby radicalizing future terrorists and contributing to further bloodshed and instability.

Nonetheless, it is easy to relate military power to political ends once a clearly articulated objective is defined. Policymakers also need to understand that strategy is a dynamic, not a static, process. Wars, particularly long ones, rarely end with the victors achieving their initial goals. The means employed by a state at any given time have to be reassessed constantly. This sets a tough challenge for any democracy, given the constraints imposed, for example, by electoral cycles. This problem is evident in counterterrorism as it is in any other type of conflict.[292] For an MACP example, Operation BANNER shows how the British state struggled with the employment of military force in pursuit of its objectives. The Army-led policy of the early 1970s that antagonized the Catholic populace gave way to police primacy after 1976. Preemptive intervention operations by 22SAS and the RUC during the late 1980s-early 1990s, such as Loughgall, were apparently directed against elements of PIRA that were the most intransigent in their commitment to the armed struggle, notably the East Tyrone Brigade. Similar operations appear to have been subsequently conducted in a less-lethal manner in order not to disrupt negotiations leading toward a peace settlement; for example, the fact that the Armagh sniper team was captured alive in April 1997 suggests that the British did not want to disrupt the peace negotiations with *Sinn Fein*'s leadership that ultimately led to PIRA's ceasefire. The deescalation process between the Army and PIRA's Derry Brigade in Londonderry during the 1990s, based on discreet contacts facilitated by Quaker intermediaries, also illustrates the flexibility of British military tactics on Operation BANNER. After a faltering start by the British in 1969-72, one can see the evolution of a process in which military force was employed to shape an eventual political outcome, namely, to encourage and coerce the Republican movement to pursue its objectives through the ballot box as opposed to the Armalite rifle and the bomb.[293]

The question of how to determine strategic priorities is evident with reference to U.S. policy in Afghanistan. Prior to the President's announcement on December 1, 2009, that an extra 30,000 troops would be sent on COIN operations in that country, the Obama administration was engaged in a prolonged debate, with Vice President Joseph Biden proposing that UAV strikes, Special Forces raids, and the use of local proxies would have a greater effect on the war against al-Qaeda and the Taliban in both Pakistan and Afghanistan than the continued COIN campaign. Both Andrew Bacevich and Austin Long are vocal proponents of this counterterrorist alternative; Long has even produced detailed recommendations of the force structure involved, concluding that 13,000 U.S. and allied elite troops and supporting personnel, complete with air assets, can contain al-Qaeda and its affiliates through a series of intelligence-led raids, assisted by the numerous Afghan tribal militias that are hostile to the Taliban and external militants. Long's argument is that such an approach will be far less expensive in blood and treasure to the United States, and will also achieve a greater economy of force, disrupting and crippling al-Qaeda and affiliated groups in Afghanistan.[294]

On closer analysis, the counterterrorism option looks less appealing. As far as its overall strategic rationale is concerned, it is fair to comment, as Michael J. Boyle has, that "[a counterterrorist] mission would focus exclusively on Al-Qaeda, while offering little or no support to the [Afghan government]; a COIN mission envisages a comprehensive commitment to defeating the Taliban and rebuilding the Afghan state while destroying Al-Qaeda operatives there."[295] A counterterrorist focus would achieve at best a tactical effect; it might eliminate substantial numbers of al-Qaeda militants, but it would not address the wider problem that Afghanistan's instability poses for regional security. It would essentially represent a refinement of the policy that successive U.S. administrations followed toward that country prior to September 2001.[296] Many of the weaknesses that Long notes in the COIN campaign could conceivably apply to his proposals. The deaths in combat of Delta Force or SEAL operators on a counterterrorist mission could have as damaging an effect on U.S. public opinion as the deaths of Soldiers and Marines in COIN operations, undermining Washington DC's will to maintain the mission in the face of popular outcry. Furthermore, Long appears to be overly confident in the ability of U.S. and allied personnel to gain accurate intelligence on al-Qaeda and like-minded militant groups from Afghan warlords and tribal leaders, particularly given the past tendency of their number to either issue false tip-offs to coalition intelligence or to accept bribes from the enemy.[297] In this respect, if U.S. and allied air strikes or Special Forces raids end up claiming innocent lives due to compromised intelligence, then their operations will have the same adverse effect on Afghan or Pakistani opinion as those reflected in recent cases in which large numbers of civilians have died due to International Security Assistance Force (ISAF) operations. It will also put further pressure on Hamid Karzai and Asif Zardari to distance their governments from U.S. actions, undermining the rationale of the counterterrorist campaign as a result.[298]

With reference to Afghanistan counterterrorism as envisaged by Bacevich and Long, it has many of the flaws of the COIN strategy; in this respect, the only alternatives for the United States and other NATO countries involved in Operation ENDURING FREEDOM are to continue with counterinsurgency and state building, or to disengage and withdraw. While operations in Iraq suggest that there is a role for elite units to decapitate terrorist adversaries such as AQI through targeted killings and intelligence-led preemptive intervention raids, it is easy to forget that these Special Forces operations required framework activity by over 150,000 U.S. troops at the height of the surge in 2007-08, in addition to a further 577,000 Iraqi troops and police. Secondly, counterterrorism is about more than using door-kickers and UAVs to eliminate high-value targets; the big disadvantage with the latter is that dead terrorists yield less HUMINT than live ones under interrogation. Whether in a domestic context, particularly with hostage rescue or with reference to a COIN campaign, there is scope for military activity to eliminate or arrest the most hardened of terrorists and insurgents. Yet, these are tactical actions that have to be integrated within a wider strategy that incorporates political, socioeconomic, cultural and information operation calculations aimed at containing terrorist violence, frustrating the objectives of the groups involved, and facilitating a peaceful settlement.[299] The Northern Ireland examples noted above can be complemented with that of Cyprus in February 1959. By this point in their campaign against EOKA, the British had acquired accurate intelligence that would enable them to trap and kill General Grivas, but then-Prime Minister Harold Macmillan vetoed an operation to eliminate him on the grounds that it would lead to an upsurge of violence from the Greek-Cypriot community which would undermine negotiations for a peace settlement.[300] One of the paradoxes of counterterrorism is that there can be a strategic rationale for *not* killing an adversary, but this is an aspect a purely military approach to this activity may overlook.

Sections Three and Four discussed the ethical dimensions of counterterrorism (in terms of *jus ad bellum* and *jus in bello*) when applying military means in both an international and domestic context. As is the case in interstate warfare, there are no easy resolutions to the ethical questions raised: Is this decision to retaliate against a nonstate group or a state sponsor proportionate? Does the use of military force resolve this problem, or complicate it? How do we avoid unnecessary deaths or human suffering? Nonetheless, for a democratic state involved in counterterrorism, the worst error a government and its officials can make is to assume that what is ethical and legal automatically conflicts with what is practical and necessary. In any action—be it the interrogation of suspects, a preemptive intervention mission to apprehend terrorists, or the killing of a senior al-Qaeda figure in a UAV attack—the question "Is this morally right?" is as important to ask as "Will this work?" More often than not, an action that is unethical is also strategically counterproductive. Democratic politicians involved in anti-terrorism need to treat strategy and ethics as intertwined. Ethics without strategy leads to indecisiveness and unproductive soul-searching, while strategy without ethics simply undermines a state's reputation and cause. The Sri Lankan government's treatment of the Tamil minority, notably the plight of around 76,000 civilians still interned in army-run camps, is not only morally flawed, but it also threatens to undermine the policy of reconciliation needed to prevent the reemergence of Tamil separatism.[301]

It is also important to remember that with the debatable exception of Israel, terrorism does not pose an existential threat to democracy. Cronin observes that "except where a state overreacts or a group becomes strong enough to transition to another form of violence [such as insurgency], killing non-combatants through terrorist attacks is not a promising way of achieving strategic political ends."[302] The only examples that have achieved such goals are the cases—such as with *Irgun* and *Lehi* in Palestine in 1945-48, the FLN in Algeria, and EOKA in Cyprus—involving colonial powers who could accept defeat and withdraw without compromising essential national interests. Although the Israelis have long perceived that Palestinian terrorism threatens state survival, in practice Israel has not only outlasted the PLO's challenge to its existence, but is arguably currently in a stronger position in relation to Hamas and its external backers than they realize. With the exception of Iran, the sponsors of the Palestinian cause have essentially conceded the rights of the Israelis to statehood, as shown by the Arab League peace initiative following the Beirut summit of March 2002. Yet Israel shows an inability to relate military strength to political objectives. This is partly a product of its notoriously fractious politics, deriving from the proliferation of political parties and the challenges of coalition-building in the *Knesset*, but it is also due to the intransigence of the current *Likud*-dominated government. The challenges to a peace settlement have not emerged from one side in the Israeli-Palestinian conflict, but the current government's reluctance to accept a Palestinian state based on 1967 borders and to curtail activities such as the building of Jewish settlements in the West Bank, which would assist peace negotiations, that demonstrates a strategic incoherence on the Israeli side. Palestinian leaders are not the only ones who, to paraphrase Abba Eban, never miss an opportunity to miss an opportunity and, in this case, the inability to relate IDF operations to strategic outcomes is clear.[303]

One consolation is that if the United States and its allies have blundered in their counterterrorist policies since 9/11, then al-Qaeda's strategic performance has been lamentable. A movement that could not even establish control over the Sunni Triangle of Iraq without encouraging the local tribes to revolt against it, let alone one that forces its former supporters to condemn it for its barbarity towards fellow Muslims, is one that is unlikely to achieve its objective of a global caliphate. It is also important to recognize that al-Qaeda by itself is very much a parasitic entity. It can exploit the advantages offered by insurgency and civil strife in certain countries, such as Afghanistan, Iraq, Yemen, and Somalia, but it cannot actually *incite* these conflicts, and, in contrast with traditional insurgent movements, it has failed to generate the level of popular backing required to seize power in any Muslim country.[304] What is indeed striking about the course of the War on Terror is the inability of al-Qaeda to capitalize on its enemies' mistakes, and its persistence in committing its own. A networked terrorist group may be difficult to attack, but it is also difficult to control and direct; hence, Ayman al Zawahiri's futile plea to Zarqawi in his letter of July 9, 2005, to stop slaughtering Shia "heretics." Al-Qaeda's most glaring failure is its irrelevance in the one issue guaranteed to mobilize Arab and Muslim opinion; namely Palestine. Not only are its members derided for their failure to help the Palestinian cause, but its leadership's clumsy efforts to incorporate Palestine into their jihad have been rejected by both Fatah and Hamas. Al-Qaeda's demise cannot be declared with confidence. In the immediate future, it will continue to recruit supporters worldwide and to plot and conduct attacks across the globe, and its affiliates, particularly Pakistani groups such as LET and HUM, will continue to destabilize particular regions such as the Indian subcontinent.

But, as Cronin notes, "in ending terrorism, [the priority for the government's involved] should not be to win people's hearts and minds, but rather to amplify the natural tendency of violent groups to lose them." Al-Qaeda and its allies are certainly acting in accordance with this tendency, particularly with reference to the increasing anger within the Muslim world at the pointlessness and callousness of its suicide bombings and other atrocities.[305]

Recent historical examples demonstrate that if a democratic state uses its armed forces in a prolonged counterterrorist role (in contrast to hostage rescue or other similar ad hoc cases), the essential mission of the military cannot, and should not, be the physical destruction of terrorist organizations, but their containment and frustration. This is not to say that individual terrorists may not be killed, but that the key process in the defeat of their organization is the demoralizing effect that military and nonmilitary operations have in constraining their activities. Terrorist groups can implode under pressure, and an organization that sees attacks consistently thwarted and members arrested and imprisoned or killed in intervention operations will become progressively less effective, and may well experience internal decay and discontent. Its activists may wonder if continued violence is worthwhile, or suspect that traitors are destroying it from within. This is as true of PIRA and ETA, as it was of the ANO and its suicidal purges during the late 1980s.[306]

Kilcullen is therefore correct when he argues that the physical elimination or incarceration of terrorists is a secondary task to wider nonmilitary measures to reduce the appeal of terrorism, notably the need to work with foreign governments, civil society groups and NGOs to address socioeconomic and political problems which may radicalize potential recruits for al-Qaeda. It is also advisable following the Iraq debacle to keep direct military intervention by Western states to an absolute minimum. But as Patrick Porter notes, specific military measures can be applied if they are related to a wider process of political engagement with regional powers, and also aspects of soft power such as public diplomacy. With reference to drone strikes in the FATA, for example, specific operations (such as the killing of Mehsud and other TTP leaders) are ideally employed in conjunction with Pakistani military operations to recover control over Waziristan. Arguably, these operations should also be used in as restricted a manner as possible, so as to ensure that a failed attack which kills several civilians does not counteract increasing public anger in Pakistan at the extent of the suicide bombings and other atrocities committed by the TTP and other militant groups.[307]

Democratic governments do need to consider other means of achieving specific counterterrorist goals. For example, David Gompert argues that the U.S. armed forces should invest more effort in developing nonlethal munitions which can be employed against terrorists and insurgents, particularly in urban conflict scenarios.[308] Gompert's recommendations are likely to meet resistance from a military hierarchy which, as noted in Section Three, fears the loss of core warfighting skills that are required when facing a state-based adversary. Furthermore, in an MACP context, the use of nonlethal means by an army does not necessarily prevent civil disaffection. Catholics in Belfast and Londonderry did not respect the British Army more because it generally used CS gas and water cannons rather than live ammunition (Bloody Sunday excepted) to quell riots during the early 1970s. Furthermore, nonlethal weapons can still be deadly; as demonstrated by occasions in which British troops and RUC officers firing baton rounds killed rioters in Northern Ireland, and also by the death of hostages through exposure to an incapacitating gas in the *Nord-Ost* siege in Moscow in October 2002.

One area where alternative solutions can and should be employed is that of the aerial interception and destruction of hijacked passenger planes. The best means of preventing another 9/11 is not to order air forces to shoot down an airliner in mid-flight, but to improve airport security and prevent would-be terrorists from being in a position to take over a plane in the first place. Mohamed Atta and his 18 companions would have been thwarted if their hand luggage had been properly searched by security staff at Boston and Newark airports, and their box-cutter knives had been confiscated. Passenger jets with cockpits controlled by keypad locks—or with sky marshals armed with tasers, mace sprays, or other nonlethal arms—would also present future hijackers with a tougher target. In this case, the best defense against future aerial suicide attacks involves a global effort to coordinate enhanced security measures with airport authorities and international airlines rather than with the RAF's QRA and other similar formations. Within individual states, close cooperation is also required between the intelligence and law enforcement agencies; the lack of interdepartmental cooperation and the lamentably adversarial relationship between the FBI and the CIA had catastrophic consequences, contributing to the failure of both the Clinton and Bush administrations to thwart the 9/11 attacks.[309]

As far as diplomatic measures are concerned, the establishment of a NATO Contact Group to liaise with other governments, such as Pakistan, or security structures, such as the Shanghai Cooperation Organization (SCO), on counterterrorism and Afghanistan, would help encourage international cooperation with both problems. An advantage NATO has with its struggle against the Taliban is that none of Afghanistan's neighbors, with the possible exception of elements within the Pakistani military and ISI, actually want to see Mullah Omar and his movement back in power. Much of the friction in the West's relationships with Russia and China could be assuaged by assurances that NATO will leave its bases in Central Asia once the Afghan government has sufficient means to fight the Taliban insurgency with a minimum of foreign support. With the remaining state sponsors of terrorist groups, the example of Libya in December 2003 suggests that diplomatic engagement, combined with sanctions and other nonviolent tools of coercion, can cajole leaders like Gaddafi into abandoning support for terrorism. Damascus's support for Hamas and other Palestinian rejectionists may diminish if Syria were to recover the Golan Heights as part of a peace deal. However, the failed attempts by U.S. officials during the late 1990s to encourage the Taliban regime to abandon its alliance with bin Laden's network show that diplomacy cannot guarantee success in persuading a state sponsor of terrorism to abandon a proxy, although it is debatable whether any regime will allow a nonstate organization to usurp its sovereignty and authority in the way that Mullah Omar did with al-Qaeda.

On an international level, Western assistance in training indigenous military and police forces has its utility, but should be provided in conjunction with discreet diplomatic pressure to introduce political and socioeconomic reforms in countries such as Pakistan, Yemen, and Uzbekistan, not to mention measures to reduce corruption and improve governance.[310] The Uzbek regime poses a particular challenge because of Karimov's despotism, not to mention the fact that Western diplomatic pressure on Tashkent can be countered by Russia and China, as neither of these states shows any particular concern about the democratic or the human rights credentials of potential allies. Yet a combination of patience and guile can and should be used by U.S. and NATO partners to encourage the Uzbek president to at least clean up his government and improve the socioeconomic plight of his subjects. Karimov's implicit threat to sabotage Operation ENDURING FREEDOM can be countered, insofar as if NATO fails in Afghanistan, his IMU foes will be the main beneficiaries. A resurgence of Islamist insurgencies across Central Asia may be, at present, a remote prospect, but it poses a potentially mortal threat to the ruling elites in Uzbekistan and neighboring states. Self-preservation and pragmatism suggest that Uzbekistan's president may not be converted to democracy overnight, but he can be persuaded that the best way of avoiding the fate of the Shah of Iran would be to stop treating his country as a private bank/torture chamber. Western governments providing military aid to Uzbekistan have more leverage over the latter than they realize.

Pakistan has also been a problematic ally not only because of its own problems with corruption and governance— although Musharraf was less greedy and more humane than his Uzbek counterpart— but also because of the self-destructive notion prevalent within the Pakistani Army and ISI hierarchy, which considers the Taliban and groups such as LET and

HUM as strategic assets regarding Kashmir and Afghanistan. Pakistan's military elite has until recently labored under the illusion that there are bad militants associated with al-Qaeda, and good militants who can be counted upon to establish a pro-Pakistani regime in Kabul (the Afghan Taliban) and to wage a proxy war in Kashmir that weakens the eternal enemy, India. A state's strategic culture cannot be changed overnight, but it appears as though the majority of Pakistanis have finally realized that jihadist and Taliban proxies actually destabilize their country; hence, widespread popular support for the Pakistani Army's counteroffensive against the TTP.[311] While this is a welcome development, American and Western aid should also be directed at specific social reforms as well as to the Pakistani security forces. Funding aimed at the provision of a more comprehensive educational system would, in the long term, do much to undermine the radical Islamist cause. If poorer Pakistanis have adequate secular schools to send their children to as opposed to *madrassas*, this would be as beneficial a development for state stability as arms supplies and training programs for the Army, police, and Frontier Corps.[312]

What of specific military measures in support of counterterrorism? On an international level, retaliation should be considered as a last resort, and regime change directed against a state sponsor is a rarity. Taliban-ruled Afghanistan was a unique case, insofar as it is extremely unlikely that any other government would allow its policies to be dictated by both an uncompromising ideology and a complete ignorance of the international environment. Prior to 9/11, Mullah Omar was warned by the U.S. Government that he would be held responsible for al-Qaeda's actions because of his willingness to provide the latter with

sanctuary and official support. Retaliation and targeted killings run the risk of provoking wider diplomatic
crises and military clashes with the states involved, as
was the case with Israel and its Arab neighbors, Turkey and Iraqi Kurdistan, and the United States with its
Special Forces raid into Pakistan in September 2008.
Hostage rescue missions require host-nation support
to be successful, Entebbe being the sole exception, and
maritime or air interdiction requires actionable intelligence to be effective.

In the domestic sphere, military means can be used
with MACA, in particular in MACP scenarios where
terrorism coexists with a wider threat to state stability.
The challenge here is to ensure that military intervention is a short-term process, akin to that of the Canadian Forces in the October crisis of 1970, rather than a
prolonged operation such as in Northern Ireland, although, depending on specific political and social circumstances, this could be easier said than done. While
the British Army's conduct in the first years of Operation BANNER has received justifiable criticism, in this
case the military faced the consequence of generations
of Catholic-Protestant strife which had brought Ulster
to the brink of civil war. As Thomas Hennessey notes,
the deterioration of the security situation in Northern
Ireland during the early 1970s was not solely a product of military ineptitude and maltreatment of the
Catholic population; it also derived from the polariza-
tion of political opinion and the decision by Republican and Loyalist groups to resort to arms to achieve
their goals.[313]

Deterrence operations have their utility, although
the deployment of troops to Heathrow in 2003 did
cause some public alarm. After Mumbai, governments operating in 2008 needed to seriously consider

the possibility of copy-cat attacks, and in the UK's case, the 2012 Olympics in London present a golden opportunity for any terrorist organization to launch a spectacular attack that would command international attention and cause widespread public panic.[314] One would hope that the contingency planning for 2012 will involve consideration of cases where the British armed forces can be swiftly deployed in the event of a major emergency, whether to contain a crisis with the deployment of military Quick Reaction Forces to cordon off a terrorist incident, or to intervene in a hostage-taking/siege scenario.

The principal conclusion here is to argue that there is a role for a state's armed forces in counterterrorism even by democracies, but that the use of military force must form part of an overall strategy which also incorporates and prioritizes nonmilitary means. For their part, both the academic community and informed opinion in general should understand that democratic governments may be required as guarantors of national security to employ their armed forces in specific circumstances, which may be beyond the capabilities of the civilian authorities. Nonetheless, governments need to ensure that the resort to armed force does not dislocate or dictate counterterrorist policy, and that the use of the military does not undermine the constitutional and legal framework upon which a liberal democracy rests. Papers of this type usually end with a list of recommendations relevant to policymakers and professional military officers. However, one of the primary points here is that any government's response to this problem depends very much on the nature of the terrorist group and the threat that it poses to the state and society. Any conclusions drawn can therefore only be generic, and in this respect, the author feels that there is more utility in concluding with a list of questions which policymakers of any liberal democratic state (be they in a Cabinet, National Security Council, or an equivalent body) need to address when faced with the complex phenomenon that is terrorism:

- Is this a domestic or an international problem?
- Are existing means (police, judiciary, and intelligence services) insufficient to deal with the threat?
- Can your chiefs of staff confirm that armed forces have the resources, manpower, and skills needed to address this specific problem?
- Would the use of the armed forces be a short-term measure (hostage-rescue, MACA, MACC, preemptive intervention, or retaliation), or will it require a long-term commitment of manpower and resources (MACP, intervention, and regime change)?
- Do opposition parties and the general public support the involvement of the military in counterterrorism?

On a domestic level:

- How effective are the terrorists, as far as both their ability to kill and injure substantial numbers of your citizens and to disrupt civil society are concerned?
- Does terrorism coexist with a major threat to state stability (such as insurgency or civil strife)?
- What precisely is the military's position within the counterterrorist hierarchy? Which authorities are the armed forces accountable to?
- How will information be gathered and disseminated between the military, the police and the

intelligence services, and who is in charge of coordinating the overall intelligence-gathering effort?

- What ROE do service personnel work under? Have you ensured that your troops operate under LOAC?
- Do the armed forces have the training needed not only to perform their duties, but also to interact effectively and in sympathy with the public in a manner that does not arouse fear or resentment among civilians?
- Regarding terrorist suspects, what guidelines are offered to military and/or police personnel responsible for their custody? Are regulations on interrogation compatible with international law and, in particular, the Geneva Convention? Does the state have procedures designed to ensure that the interrogation of terrorist suspects for intelligence purposes minimize the dangers that the latter might be maltreated?
- Has the government planned and rehearsed responses to specific contingencies through war games, command post exercises, etc.? Have these been conducted with all the relevant agencies?
- Have shortcomings and problems in these exercises been identified and an attempt made to resolve them (relating to bureaucratic parameters, chain of command, and other logistical and organizational complications)?
- In circumstances short of an imminent and dire emergency, such as a major terrorist incident requiring an immediate MACC response, has the government consulted the parliamentary

opposition on its reasons for calling out the armed forces?

On an international level:
- Do other governments support your resort to armed force? If so, will they cooperate in either providing their own military units in a coalition, or by other means (sharing intelligence, providing host-nation support and bases, etc.)?
- Can military action be justified under international law?
- If you are intervening on the territory of another sovereign state, is that country's government sympathetic to the terrorists? Are you retaliating against the terrorist organization itself, or the regime that supports it?
- If, in the scenario described above, the indigenous government is not aligned with the terrorists, can it be persuaded to take action against the latter itself?
- Is it more politically sensitive and practical to provide indirect assistance to indigenous security forces (e.g. training, arms, intelligence cooperation, or air support) in their own counterterrorist campaign?
- If you are involved in training local security forces, can you ensure that they are employed in the roles you intend rather than for more nefarious purposes (such as a praetorian guard for a repressive regime, or as a death squad)? In this instance, what mechanisms do you have to prevent them from "going rogue"?
- If you are assisting a third-party government, can you also influence it to introduce the necessary socioeconomic and governance reforms

that address the grievances which contribute to terrorist activity?

- Will the commitment of your armed forces overseas deprive you of the means needed to respond effectively to a domestic MACA emergency?
- Is a foreign intervention mission likely to be so controversial that it antagonizes or even radicalizes a section of your own society?
- Finally, if you are trying to overthrow a regime that supports terrorism, such as the Taliban, do you have international opinion on your side? Are you also prepared for the long-term stabilization and state-building effort that will inevitably follow regime change?

ENDNOTES

1. Julian Borger, "David Miliband expands on criticism of 'war on terror' phase," *The Guardian*, January 15, 2009. The author's attempt to find a transcript of Miliband's speech on the Foreign and Commonwealth Office website produced a dead link: *www.fco. gov.uk/en/newsroom/latest-news/?view=Speech&id=12175593*.

2. *Ibid.*

3. Angela Rabasa *et al.*, *The Lessons of Mumbai*, Santa Monica, CA: RAND, 2009, p. 5.

4. Rahul Bedi, "Country Briefing: India," *Jane's Defence Weekly (JDW)*, Vol. 46, No. 3, January 21, 2009; *Dispatches – Terror in Mumbai*, broadcast on Channel 4, June 30, 2009. Only one of the attackers, Mohamed Ajmal Amir Qasab, was captured alive and put on trial, receiving a death sentence for his part in the atrocity. "Mumbai attack gunman Qasab sentenced to death," BBC News, May 6, 2010, available from *www.news.bbc.co.uk/1/hi/world/south_ asia?8664179.stm*.

5. Speech by President Barack Obama, March 27, 2009, emphasis added; available from *www.cbsnews.com/blogs/2009/03/27/politics/politicalhotsheet/entry4896758.shtml*.

6. "Mme Clinton; le but est d 'éradiquer' Al-Qaida" ("Mrs. Clinton: The mission is to 'eradicate' Al-Qaeda"), *Le Monde*, November 17, 2009.

7. "Barack Obama rallies forces on visit to Afghanistan," BBC News, March 29, 2010, available from *news.bbc.co.uk/1/hi/world/south_asia/8591866.stm*; Alice Fordham, "Terror suspect's father asks U.S. court to ban CIA from killing 'al-Qaeda' son," *The Times*, August 27, 2010.

8. Lolita C. Baldor, "Pentagon seeks billions to battle terror abroad," *Washington Post*, February 4, 2010; David Ignatius, "What the partisan squabbles miss on Obama's terror response," *Washington Post*, February 17, 2010.

9. John Hutton, Speech at Institute of Public Policy Research, London, UK, April 27, 2009, available from *www.acronym.org/docs/0904/doc13.htm*; Sean Rayment, "SAS and other Special Forces to be expanded to defeat al Qaeda," *Daily Telegraph* April 25, 2009.

10. Reza Aslan, "Losing the 'War on Terror'," *Los Angeles Times*, April 8, 2009.

11. Professor Geras's examination of FKATWOT is available from *normblog.typepad.com/normblog/2009/02/fkatwot-index.html*.

12. For critical analyses of the War on Terror, see Seymour Hersh, *Chain of Command*, London, UK: Penguin, 2005; and Philippe Sands, *Lawless World. Making and Breaking Global Rules*, London, UK: Penguin, 2006.

13. Jesse Norman, "Tensions of Terrorism," *The World Today*, August/September, 2005, pp. 22-24; Rohan Gunaratna, "An examination of Al-Qaeda and its methods," *Intersec*, Vol. 15, No. 3, 2005, pp. 85-87; Conor Gearty, "Dilemmas of Terror," *Prospect Magazine*, October, 2007, pp. 34-38.

14. Ahmed Rashid, *Descent into Chaos. The World's Most Unstable Region and the Threat to Global Security,* London, UK: Penguin, 2009, pp. xlvii-xlviii.

15. David Kilcullen, *The Accidental Guerrilla: Fighting Small Wars in the Midst of a Big One,* London, UK: C. Hurst, 2009, pp. 274-275, 284-286; Aslan; "Remarks by the President at Cairo University," June 4, 2009, available from *www.whitehouse.gov/the_press_office/Remarks-by-the-President-at-Cairo-University-6-04-09/.*

16. Prime examples of journalistic commentary can be seen in Simon Jenkins, "The 'War on Terror' licenses a new stupidity in geopolitics," *The Guardian,* January 30, 2008; and Gary Younge, "Time for Barack Obama to retire not only the term 'War on Terror,' but the war itself," *The Guardian,* September 14, 2009.

17. George Kassimeris, "Introduction," in George Kassimeris, ed., *Playing Politics with Terrorism: A User's Guide,* London, UK: C. Hurst, 2007, pp. 11-12.

18. Barbara Elias, ed., "The Taliban File Part IV," *National Security Archive Electronic Briefing Book,* No.134, August 18, 2005, available from *www.gwu.edu/~nsarchiv/NASEBB/NSAEBB134/index2.htm*; Michael J. Boyle, "Do counterterrorism and counterinsurgency go together," *International Affairs,* Vol. 86, No. 2, 2010, p. 342.

19. G. Davidson Smith, "Military Options in Response to State-Sponsored Terrorism," *Terrorism and Political Violence,* Vol. 1, No. 3, 1989, pp. 294-323. See also Paul Wilkinson, *Terrorism Versus Democracy: The Liberal State Response,* London, UK: Frank Cass, 2001, pp. 102-105, 124-136.

20. Ghaith Abdul-Ahad, "The invisible war: How Somalia's unending conflict became the new front in the battle against al-Qaida," *The Guardian,* June 8, 2010; Joshua Keating, "Pirates or terrorists? Pick your poison," *Foreign Policy,* May 4, 2010, available from *www.foreignpolicy.com/posts/2010/05/04/pirates_or_terrorists_pick_your_poison.*

21. Hew Strachan, "Making Strategy: Civil-Military Relations after Iraq," *Survival,* Vol. 48, No. 3, 2006, pp. 59-60; Jeremy Pressman, "Power without Influence: The Bush Administration's For-

eign Policy Failure in the Middle East," *International Security*, Vol. 33, No. 4, 2009, pp. 149-179.

22. Raffaello Pantucci, "Deep Impact: The effect of drone attacks on British counter-terrorism," *RUSI Journal*, Vol. 154, No. 5, 2009, p. 72.

23. Cerwyn Moore and David Barnard-Wills, "Russia and counter-terrorism. A critical appraisal," in Asaf Siniver, ed., *International Terrorism Post-9/11. Comparative Dynamics and Responses*, Abingdon, UK: Routledge, 2010, pp. 144-167.

24. Kilcullen, p. 181. This is not to say that the British Army and colonial security forces did not commit abuses against the Greek Cypriot population. See Panagiotis Dimitrakis, "British Intelligence and the Cyprus Insurgency, 1955-1959," *International Journal of Intelligence and Counterintelligence*, Vol. 21, No. 2, 2008, p. 381. For the respective strengths and weaknesses of history and political science methodology, see Paul W. Schroeder, "History and International Relations Theory: Not Use or Abuse, but Fit or Misfit," *International Security*, Vol. 22, No. 1, 1997, pp. 64-74.

25. Jason Burke, "Saudis offer pioneering therapy for ex-jihadis," *The Guardian*, March 9, 2008. The effectiveness of these methods has been questioned. See "An awful lot," *The Economist*, July 25, 2009.

26. Ahmed Rashid, *Jihad. The Rise of Militant Islam in Central Asia*, New Haven, CT: Yale University Press, 2002, pp. 137-186; "The blood red revolution," *The Economist*, May 21, 2005; "Fata Fergana," *The Economist*, June 13, 2009.

27. James Sanders, *Apartheid's Friends. The Rise and Fall of South Africa's Secret Services*, London, UK: John Murray, 2006, pp. 198-226, 255-281; Paul Lewis, *Guerrillas and Generals. The "Dirty War" in Argentina*, Westport CT: Praeger, 2002.

28. Michael Hastings, "The Runaway General," *Rolling Stone*, June 22, 2010, available from *www.rollingstone.com/politics/news/17390/119236*; "More than a one-man problem," *The Economist* 26th June, 2010; Thomas Rid & Thomas Keaney, "Counterinsurgency in Context," in Thomas Rid & Thomas Keaney, ed., *Un-*

derstanding Counterinsurgency: Doctrine, Operations and Challenges, London, UK: Routledge, 2010, pp. 256-257.

29. "The bombs of August," *The Economist*, August 21, 2010.

30. For U.S. and British examples, see *Field Manual (FM) 3-24, Counterinsurgency*, Washington DC: Department of the Army, 2006; *Field Manual (FM) 3-07, Stability Operations*, Washington, DC: Department of the Army, 2008; *Joint Publication (JP) 3-40, Security and Stabilization: The Military Contribution*, London, UK: Ministry of Defence (MOD), 2010.

31. Audrey Kurth Cronin, *How Terrorism Ends: Understanding the Decline and Demise of Terrorist Campaigns*, Princeton NJ: Princeton University Press, 2009, p. 25.

32. For explanations as to how terrorist campaigns end (with reference to the degree to which these are due to state strategies to defeat said organizations), see Audrey Kurth Cronin, *Ending Terrorism: Lessons for defeating al-Qaeda*, Adelphi Paper No. 394, 2008. See also Cronin, *How Terrorism Ends*.

33. Colin Gray, *War, Peace and International Relations: An Introduction to Strategic Theory*, London, UK: Routledge, 2007, p. 236; Jim Dorschner, "Mission fatigue: The future of military intervention," *Jane's Intelligence Review (JIR)*, Vol. 6, No. 19, 2007, pp. 31-35. Out of 192 UN member states, only 27 have no armed forces. See *www.demilitarisation.com/Countrieswithoutarmy.htm*.

34. Andrew McGregor, "Turkey's Gendarmerie: Reforming a Frontline Unit in the War on Terrorism," *Jamestown Foundation Terrorism Monitor (JFTM)*, Vol. 6, No. 22, November 25, 2008; Mark Galeotti, "Russia's Interior Troops on the Rise," *JIR*, Vol. 9, No. 6, 1997, pp. 243-246; Rahul Bedi, "Kashmir's Future," *JIR*, Vol. 7, No. 7, 1995, pp. 324-328.

35. Bob Woodward, "Secret CIA Units Playing a Central Combat Role," *Washington Post*, November 18, 2001; Jeremy Page, "Google Earth reveals secret history of U.S. base in Pakistan," *The Times*, February 19, 2009; Tom Coghlan, "CIA caught in a dirty and secretive war against al-Qaeda on Afghan border," *The Times*, January 1, 2010.

36. Jeremy Scahill, "Blackwater's Secret War in Pakistan," *The Nation*, November 23, 2009, available from *www.thenation.com/doc/20091207/scahill.print*.

37. Fareed Zakaria, "The Rise of Illiberal Democracy," *Foreign Affairs*, Vol. 76, No. 6, 1997, pp. 22-43; "Coups away," *The Economist*, February 13, 2010.

38. *Ibid.* The 19th century French political thinker Alexis de Tocqueville believed that "democracy" and "liberty" were not necessarily synonymous. See Larry Siedentop, *Tocqueville* (OUP 1994) for an explanation of his ideas.

39. Vanora Bennett, *Crying Wolf. The Return of War to Chechnya*, New York: Macmillan, 2001, pp. 26-27, pp. 111-113; James Hughes, "Chechnya: The Causes of a Protracted Post-Soviet Conflict," *Civil Wars*, Vol. 4, No. 4, 2001, p. 16.

40. Magnus Ranstorp and Paul Wilkinson, "Introduction: International Conference on Terrorism and Human Rights," *Terrorism and Political Violence*, Vol. 17, No. 1, 2005, pp. 3-4.

41. Charles Townshend, *Terrorism: A Very Short Introduction*, Oxford, UK: Oxford University Press (OUP), 2002, p. 134; Alex P. Schmid, "Terrorism and Democracy," in Alex P. Schmid and Roland Crelinstein, eds., *Western Responses to Terrorism*, London, UK: Frank Cass, 1993, pp. 14-19.

42. Afua Hirsch, "David Davis warns MPs of erosion of civil liberties," *The Guardian*, February, 20, 2009; John Newsinger, *British Counter-Insurgency*, Basingstoke, UK: Palgrave, 2002, p. 101; Alistair Horne, *A Savage War of Peace. Algeria 1954-1962*, New York: Macmillan, 1996, pp. 232-236; "Hearts and Minds," *The Economist*, November 14, 2009.

43. Bruce Hoffman, *Inside Terrorism*, 2nd Ed., New York: Columbia University Press, 2006, pp. 1-41. For a survey of terrorism's evolution, see Michael Burleigh, *Blood and Rage. A Cultural History of Terrorism*, London, UK: HarperCollins, 2009; Randall Law, *Terrorism: A History*, Cambridge, UK: Polity Press, 2009.

44. Frantz Fanon, *The Wretched of the Earth*, London, UK: MacGibbon & Kee, 1965.

45. See, for example, Noam Chomsky, "The United States is a Leading Terrorist State," *Monthly Review*, Vol. 53, No. 6, 2001, available from *www.monthlyreview.org/1101Chomsky.htm*; William Blum, *Rogue State: A Guide to the World's Only Superpower*, London, UK: Zed Books, 2006; and Fanon.

46. Lawrence Freedman, "Terrorism as a Strategy," *Government and Opposition*, Vol. 42, No. 3, 2007, p. 319.

47. Hoffman, *Inside Terrorism*, pp. 22-27, 258-264; Freedman, p. 319.

48. Daniel Byman, *Deadly Connections: States that Sponsor Terrorism*, Cambridge, UK: Cambridge University Press, 2005, pp. 22, 37-38; Ed Moloney, *A Secret History of the IRA*, New York: Penguin, 2003, p. 14.

49. Norman Davies, *Heart of Europe. A Short History of Poland*, OUP, 1986, pp. 18-19, 392-393, 405-407, 416; Ranstorp and Wilkinson, "Terrorism and Human Rights," p. 6; Freedman, "Terrorism as a Strategy," pp. 334-335.

50. Editorial, "Despite confession, Kasab remains 'gunman' for NYT," *The Times of India*, July 26, 2009.

51. Wilkinson, *Terrorism Versus Democracy*, pp. 1, 19; Nick van der Bijl, *Operation Banner. The British Army in Northern Ireland 1969-2007*, Barnsley, UK: Pen and Sword Books, 2009, pp. 188-190; Peter Taylor, "Six days that shook Britain," *The Guardian*, July 24, 2002; *SAS: Embassy Siege*, broadcast on BBC2 on July 25, 2002.

52. Lawrence Wright, *The Looming Tower*, New York: Penguin, 2007, pp. 270-272. Both bombs were delivered by trucks driven by suicide attackers. The Nairobi blast killed 213 people (12 Americans, the rest Kenyan) and wounded 4,500 more. The Dar es-Salaam attack killed 11 Tanzanians and wounded 85 Tanzanian and U.S. citizens.

53. Hoffman, *Inside Terrorism*, pp. 38-40, 285-289.

54. Brian Jenkins, "International Terrorism: A Balance Sheet," *Survival*, Vol. 17, No. 4, 1975, p. 158.

55. John Arquilla and David Ronfeldt, "The Advent of Netwar (Revisited)," in Arquilla and Ronfeldt, eds., *Networks and Netwars: The Future of Terror, Crime and Militancy*, Santa Monica, CA: RAND Corporation, 2001, pp. 1-25.

56. Hoffman, *Inside Terrorism*, pp. 38-40, 285-289; Moloney, *IRA*, pp. 376-377, 573; Arquilla and Ronfeldt, "The Advent of Netwar, Revisited."

57. Readers may be reminded here of Colonel "Philippe Mathieu" and his dissection of the FLN infrastructure in Gillo Pontecorvo's film, *The Battle of Algiers* (1966).

58. Bard O'Neill, *Insurgency and Terrorism*, London, UK: Brassey's, 1990, p. 13; Sherifa Zuhur, *Hamas and Israel: Conflicting Strategies of Group-Based Politics*, Carlisle PA: Strategic Studies Institute, U.S. Army War College, December, 2008, available from *www.fas.org/man/eprint/zuhur.pdf*.

59. Jon Lee Anderson, *Guerrillas*, New York: HarperCollins 1992, pp. 68-85; Kilcullen, p. 223. Christopher Tuck, "Northern Ireland and the British Approach to Counter-Insurgency," *Defence & Security Analysis*, Vol. 23, No. 2, 2007, pp. 168-169.

60. Ahmed Hashim, *Insurgency and Counterinsurgency in Iraq*, London, UK: C. Hurst, 2006; Hans Klepak, "Colombia: Why doesn't the war end?," *JIR*, Vol. 12, No. 6, 2000, pp. 41-45; Jerome Taylor, "Tamil Tigers: Defeated at Home, Defiant Abroad," *The Independent*, May 23, 2009; "The Corpse of the Tigers," *The Economist*, May 23, 2009.

61. Peter Bergen and Katherine Tiedemann, "The Drone War," *The New Republic*, June 3, 2009; "Profile: Baitullah Mehsud," BBC News, August 8, 2009, available from *news.bbc.co.uk/go/pr/ fr/-/1/hi/world/south_asia/7163626.stm*; Amir Rana, "Enemy of the state—Lashkar-e-Jhangvi and militancy in Pakistan," *JIR*, Vol. 21, No. 9, 2009, pp. 14-19.

62. FM 3-24, pp. 1-1 - 1-29; *Army Field Manual (AFM) 1-10, Counter Insurgency Operations, Strategic and Operational Guidelines*, Rev. Ed., London, UK: MOD, 2007, pp. A-2-1, B-3-1. "Counterterrorism" has been interpreted as the use of state terror to intimi-

date a population that shelters terrorists. See Law, *Terrorism: A History*, p. 7; and Townshend, *Terrorism*, pp. 114-115. But this author defines counterterrorism as all measures a state may take, of varying degrees of discrimination and legitimacy, in its defense. The British Army COIN manual is available from *wikileaks.org/wiki/Wikileaks*. The U.S. manual was published by the University of Chicago Press in, 2007.

63. Geraint Hughes and Christian Tripodi, "Anatomy of a Surrogate: Historical Precedents and Implications for Contemporary Counter-insurgency and Counter-terrorism," *Small Wars and Insurgencies*, Vol., 20, No. 1, 2009, pp. 7-10.

64. A copy of the "Yellow Card" can be found in FCO87/584, the National Archives, UK, NAUK. Also see Donald Macintyre, "Israel's death squad: A soldier's story," *The Independent*, March 1, 2009; General Paul Aussaresses, *The Battle of the Casbah*, New York: Enigma Books, 2006; Horne, *Savage War of Peace*, pp. 183-207.

65. *The Strategic Defence Review: A New Chapter*, London, UK: The Stationary Office, 2002; *Defence White Paper, 2003: Delivering Security in a Changing World*, London, UK: The Stationary Office, 2003.

66. *The United Kingdom's Strategy for Countering International Terrorism*, London, UK: The Stationary Office, 2009, p. 8.

67. Warren Chin, "The United Kingdom and the War on Terror: The Breakdown of National and Military Strategy," *Contemporary Security Policy*, Vol. 30, No. 1, 2009, pp. 127-128, 141; *Strategy for Countering International Terrorism*.

68. M. L. R. Smith and Sophie Roberts, "War in the Gray: Exploring the concept of Dirty War," *Studies in Conflict & Terrorism (SC&T)*, Vol. 31, No. 5, 2008, pp. 385-388. Examples of enhanced anti-terrorist legislation include the introduction of the Diplock Courts in Northern Ireland in 1972, where juries were abolished because its members faced intimidation, and the Prevention of Terrorism Bill of November 1974. See van der Bijl, *Operation Banner*, pp. 76-77, 117.

69. Hughes, "Chechnya," p. 37; Mark Kramer, "The Perils of Counterinsurgency: Russia's war in Chechnya," *International Security*, Vol. 29, No. 3, 2004-05, pp. 57-58; Tracey German, *Russia's Chechen War*, London, UK: Routledge, 2003, pp. 151-154.

70. Cronin, *How Terrorism Ends*, p. 116.

71. William C. Banks, "Troops Defending the Homeland: The Posse Comitatus Act and the Legal Environment for a Military Role in Domestic Counter-Terrorism," *Terrorism and Political Violence*, Vol. 14, No. 3, 2002, pp. 1-41. *Posse Comitatus* does not apply to the U.S. Coast Guard, which is one of the five U.S. armed services, but has a law enforcement mandate. It is currently under the jurisdiction of the Department of Homeland Security, not the Department of Defense, see *www.uscg.mil/top/missions/*.

72. Meliton Cardona, "The European Response to Terrorism," in Schmid and Crelinstein, *Western Responses to Terrorism*, p. 260. George Kassimeris, *Europe's Last Red Terrorists: The Revolutionary Organisation 17th November*, New York: New York University Press, 2001.

73. A good survey of leftist terrorism in West Germany can be found on *This is Baader-Meinhoff*, a website maintained by Richard Huffman, available from *www.baader-meinhoff.com*.

74. Townshend, *Terrorism*, p. 69. The quote from Dalla Chiesa comes from Alan Dershowitz, *Why Terrorism Works*, New Haven, CT: Yale University Press, 2003, p. 134. Dershowitz argues that Moro's subsequent death invalidated these remarks. The author believes instead that the General's refusal to contemplate police-state measures actually helped preserve Italian democracy against a resort to authoritarianism and state terror. The Moro Affair did inspire conspiracy theories proclaiming that the Italian establishment had connived in his murder. For an analysis and rebuttal, see Richard Drake, "The Aldo Moro Murder Case in Retrospect," *Journal of Cold War Studies*, Vol. 8, No. 2, 2006, pp. 114-125.

75. Clive Jones cites a total of 1,030 Israelis and 3,529 Palestinians killed between September 2000 and January 2005 in "Israel and the al-Aqsa intifada. The *Conceptzia* of Terror," in Siniver, *International Terrorism*, p. 129. The Israeli human rights group

B'Tselem gives figures of 4,745 Palestinian fatalities killed by Israel's security forces between October 2000 and December 2008, available from *www.btselem.org/English/Statistics/Casualties.asp*. As is invariably the case, the question of how many of those killed were fighters as opposed to civilians is a cause for intense controversy.

76. Daniel Benjamin and Steven Simon, *The Age of Sacred Terror*, New York: Random House, 2003, pp. 195-198. Stathis Kalyvas, "Wanton and Senseless? The Logic of Massacres in Algeria," *Rationality and Society*, Vol. 11, No. 3, 1999, pp. 243-285.

77. Holly Fletcher, "Militant Extremists in the United States," Washington, DC: Council on Foreign Relations, April 21, 2006, available from *www.cfr.org/publication/9236/*. See also the FBI Strategic Plan, 2004-2009, available from *www.fbi.gov/publications/strategicplan/stategicplantext.htm#intro*.

78. Byman, *Deadly Connections*, pp. 53-78. David Childs and Richard Popplewell, *Stasi: The East German Intelligence and Security Service*, Basingstoke, UK: Macmillan, 1996, pp. 155-158; John Schneidel, "My Enemy's Enemy: Twenty Years of Co-operation between West Germany's Red Army Faction and the GDR Ministry for State Security," *Intelligence & National Security*, Vol. 8, No. 4, 1993, pp. 54-72; Moloney, pp. 17-33.

79. Uri Bar-Noi and Rami Ginat, "Tacit Support for Terrorism: The Rapprochment between the USSR and Palestinian Guerrilla Organizations Following the 1967 War," *Journal of Strategic Studies*, Vol. 30, No. 2, 2007, pp. 255-284; Magnus Ranstorp, *Hizb'allah in Lebanon. The Politics of the Western Hostage Crisis*, Basingstoke, UK: Macmillan, 1997, pp. 33-40; *Iran and the West*, Part 2, broadcast on BBC2 on February 14, 2009.

80. Boyle, "Do counterterrorism and counterinsurgency go together," p. 344; Efraim Inbar and Shmuel Sandler, "Israel's Deterrence Strategy Revisited," *Security Studies*, Vol. 3, No. 2, 1993, pp. 330-358; Editorial, "Testing Israel's Deterrence," *Jerusalem Post*, January 28, 2009.

81. For a comprehensive account of the early phase of the Northern Ireland conflict, see Thomas Hennessey, *The Evolution of the Troubles, 1970-72*, Dublin, Ireland: Irish Academic Press,

2007; Lieutenant-General D. G. House and Chief Constable K. Newman, *Joint Directive by General Officer Commanding Northern Ireland and Chief Constable Royal Ulster Constabulary*, January 12, 1977, DEFE11/917(NAUK); Peter R. Neumann, "The Myth of Ulsterization in British Security Policy in Northern Ireland," *SC&T*, Vol. 26, No. 5, 2003, pp. 365-378.

82. Hoffman, *Inside Terrorism*, pp. 21-23. Christopher Andrew notes that *Lehi* were the last group to describe themselves as "terrorists." See *The Defence of the Realm: The Authorised History of MI5*, London, UK: Penguin, 2010, p. 351.

83. Cronin, *How Terrorism Ends*, p. 117. Khan is quoted in Chin, "War on Terror," p. 141.

84. A copy of bin Laden's *fatwa* can be found online on the Public Broadcasting Service website, available from *www.pbs.org/newshour/terrorism/international/fatwa_1998.html*; Daniel R. Morris, "Surprise and Terrorism: A Conceptual Framework," *Journal of Strategic Studies*, Vol. 32, No. 1, 2009, pp. 1-27; Barry Rubin, "The Real Roots of Arab Anti-Americanism," *Foreign Affairs*, Vol. 81, No. 6, 2002, pp. 73-85; Benjamin and Simon, *Sacred Terror*, p. 386.

85. Carl von Clausewitz, *On War*, Michael Howard and Peter Paret, eds and trans., Princeton, NJ: Princeton University Press, 1976, pp. 75-77; Cronin, *How Terrorism Ends*, pp. 4-8, 117.

86. Frank Kitson, *Bunch of Five*, London, UK: Faber and Faber, 1977, p. 283; Cronin, *How Terrorism Ends*.

87. Cronin, *How Terrorism Ends*, p. 35; Desmond Hamill, *Pig in the Middle. The Army in Northern Ireland 1969-1985*, London, UK: Methuen, 1986, pp. 268-269. Three prisoners from the Irish National Liberation Army (INLA) also died during the hunger strike. Eamon Collins (with Mick McGovern), *Killing Rage*, London, UK: Granta Books 1998, pp. 233-243; Anthony McIntyre, *Good Friday: The Death of Irish Republicanism*, New York: Ausubo Press, 2008, pp. 157-174.

88. Thomas R. Mockaitis, *The "New" Terrorism: Myths and Reality*, London, UK: Praeger, 2007, pp. 5, 7.

89. "Mowlam: We must talk to al-Qaeda," BBC News, April 8, 2004, available from *news.bbc.co.uk/1/hi/uk_politics/3611805.stm*; "Should the Government hold talks with terrorists?" *The Daily Telegraph*, March 15, 2008; Sir Francis Richards, "The development of the UK intelligence community after 9/11," Siniver, *International Terrorism*, p. 122.

90. Burleigh, *Blood and Rage*, pp. 146-151, 385-396. Despite optimistic claims to the contrary by Azzam Tamimi, Hamas has yet to produce a revised version of its 1988 Charter, with its explicitly anti-Semitic character. Orly Halpern, "Hamas working on 'new' charter," *Jerusalem Post*, February 18, 2006.

91. Robert Baer, *See No Evil*, London, UK: Arrow Books, 2002; "Israel denies assassinating Hezbollah chief," *The Daily Telegraph*, February 13, 2008.

92. Ronen Bergman, *The Secret War with Iran*, Oxford, UK: Oneworld Publications, 2008, p. 67.

93. "The jihadi who turned 'supergrass'," BBC News, September 13, 2006, available from *news.bbc.co.uk/1/hi/programmes/5334594.stm*.

94. Mockaitis, *"New" Terrorism*, p. 14; Peter R. Neumann, "Negotiating with Terrorists," *Foreign Affairs*, Vol. 86, No. 1, 2007, pp. 128-138.

95. Brian Cloughley, "Swat Team," *JIR*, Vol. 21, No. 8, 2009, pp. 14-19; Owen Bennett Jones, "On the verge: Pakistan's insecurity," *RUSI Journal*, Vol. 155, No. 1, 2010, pp. 4-8.

96. McIntyre, *Good Friday*, pp. 6-8, 293-310; Colonel Richard Iron, "Britain's Longest War: Northern Ireland 1967-2007," in Daniel Marston and Carter Malkasian, ed., *Counterinsurgency in Modern Warfare*, London, UK: Osprey, 2007, pp. 176-179; Henry McDonald, *Gunsmoke and Mirrors: How Sinn Fein Dressed up Defeat as Victory*, Dublin, Ireland: Gill & Macmillan, 2008.

97. Peter Harclerode, *Secret Soldiers: Special Forces in the War Against Terrorism*, London, UK: Cassell & Co, 2000, pp. 367-382, 507-524; *Age of Terror – Part Three*, broadcast on BBC2 on June 18,

2008; "Territorial Support Group," on Metropolitan police website, available from *www.met.police.uk/co/territorial_support.htm*.

98. Robyn Pangi, *Consequence Management in the 1995 Sarin Attacks on the Japanese Subway System*, Belfer Center for Science and International Affairs (BCSIA) Discussion Paper, 2002-4, ESDP Discussion Paper, ESDP2002-01, Cambridge, MA: Harvard University, John F. Kennedy School of Government, February, 2002, available from *belfercenter.ksg.harvard.edu/files/consequence_management_in_the_1995_sarin_attacks_on_the_japanese_subway_system.pdf*. The Sarin attack killed 12 people and injured 1,034; 50 of these were classed as severe casualties.

99. Clive Walker and James Broderick, *The Civil Contingencies Act, 2004. Risk, Resilience, and the Law in the United Kingdom*, Oxford, UK: Oxford University Press (OUP), 2006, pp. 247-250; "Stark option in frontline terror flight," BBC News, October 18, 2005, available from *news.bbc.co.uk/go/pr/fr/-/1/hi/uk/4351622.stm*. See also *www.raf.mod.uk/rafregiment/rafregimentsquadrons/27_sqn_history.cfm*.

100. Staff reporter, "Why the siege tactics had to be switched," *The Observer*, May 11, 1980; Joey Gardiner, "What is Cobra?," *The Guardian*, October 21, 2002; GEN135(72)3, *Use of the Cabinet Office Briefing Room*, November 29, 1972, CAB130/620(NAUK).

101. David Benest, "Aden to Northern Ireland, 1966-76," in Hew Strachan, ed., *Big Wars and Small Wars: The British Army and Lessons of War in the Twentieth Century*, London, UK: Routledge, 2006, pp. 115-144; Hennessey, *Troubles*; Hamill, *Pig in the Middle*; Peter Taylor, *Brits*, London, UK: Bloomsbury, 2002.

102. David Charters and James LeBlanc, "Peacekeeping and Internal Security: The Canadian Army in Low Intensity Operations," in David Charters and Maurice Tugwell, eds., *Armies in Low Intensity Conflict: A Comparative Analysis*, London, UK: Brassey's, 1989, pp. 150-154; Lieutenant General Romeo Dallaire, the UN force commander in Rwanda in 1994, witnessed the October crisis as a junior officer. See his account in *Shake Hands with the Devil*, London, UK: Arrow Books, 2005, pp. 23-27.

103. GEN129(74)first and third meetings, January 7 and 15, 1973; and GEN129(74)2, *Protection of Airports in the United Kingdom*, January 8, 1974, CAB130/636(NAUK).

104. GEN129(72)6, *Working Group on Terrorist Activities. Report to Ministers*, October 20, 1972, CAB130/616(NAUK); GEN129(74)3, *Terrorist Threat at Heathrow Airport*, January 18, 1974, CAB130/636(NAUK); Nick Hopkins and Richard Norton-Taylor, "Huge hunt for missile smugglers," *The Guardian*, February 13, 2003.

105. Bergman, *Secret War*, pp. 269-272; David Hartwell, "Ship's capture increases fear of Hizbollah," *JIR*, Vol. 21, No. 12, 2009, p. 5. One controversial example that this paper does not examine concerns the interception of the Gaza aid convoy by the IDF on May 31, 2010, which culminated in a bloody clash on the MV *Mavi Marmara* between *Shayetet* 13 and Turkish Islamist activists. The author does not examine this incident, since the IDF did not treat it as an anti-terrorist operation, but as one conducted in support of the blockade on Hamas-ruled Gaza. For a careful analysis of this contentious event, see "Death on the Med," a *Panorama* documentary broadcast on BBC1 at 8:30 p.m., August 16, 2010. See also "How Israel Plays into Hamas's Hands," *The Economist*, June 5, 2010.

106. R. A. Custis (MOD) to P. L. Gregson (MOD), April 24, 1972, DEFE11/789(NAUK); Andrew, *Defence of the Realm*, pp. 622-623, 703-704; Van der Bijl, *Operation Banner*, p. 84; Moloney, *IRA*, pp. 1-33, 460-461.

107. "Perils of the Sea," *The Economist*, April 17, 2009. Richard Scott, "Policing the maritime beat," *JDW*, Vol. 46, No. 17, April 29, 2009; Martin Murphy, *Contemporary Piracy and Maritime Terrorism: The Threat to International Security*, International Institute of Strategic Studies: Adelphi Paper No. 388, London, UK: Routledge, 2007.

108. Rashid, *Descent into Chaos*, pp. 223-224; Andrew Black, "Weapons for Warlords: Arms Trafficking in the Gulf of Aden," *JFTM*, Vol. 12, No. 17, June 18, 2009.

109. Bout was arrested in Thailand by U.S. law enforcement agents in March 2008. The latter were posing as members of FARC, and Bout is accused of planning to sell arms to this Colombian group. His extradition to the United States was announced on August 20, 2010. Andrew Osborn, "'Merchant of Death,' Viktor Bout will finally face justice," *Daily Telegraph*, August 21, 2010;

Roberto Saviano, *Gomorrah*, Virginia Jewiss, trans., London, UK: Macmillan, 2008, pp. 181-186.

110. Timothy Naftali, *Blind Spot: The Secret History of American Counterterrorism*, New York: Basic Books, 2005, pp. 171-174; "A battle between two long arms," *The Economist*, April 3, 2009.

111. Ruslan Temirov, "Uzbekistan's Army: Going Professional," *Eurasia Insight*, May 14, 2004, available from *www.eurasianet. org/departments/insight/articles/eav051404.shtml*; Alexander Cooley, "Base Politics," *Foreign Affairs*, Vol. 84, No. 6, November/December 2005, pp. 79-92.

112. Monte Morin, "U.S. Trainers Prepare Ethiopians to Fight,"*Stars and Stripes*, December 30, 2006; James J. F. Forest and Rebecca Crispin, "AFRICOM: Troubled Infancy, Promising Future," *Contemporary Security Policy*, Vol. 30, No. 1, 2009, pp. 5-27; "U.S. Military Calls Up Europe," *Africa Confidential*, Vol. 51, No. 6, March 19, 2010.

113. "U.S. training military in Sahara," BBC News, May 3, 2010, available from *news.bbc.co.uk/go/pr/fr/-/1/hi/world/africa/8658009.stm*; Martin Vogl, "Train to Gain," *JDW*, Vol. 47, No. 31, August 4, 2010.

114. Lauren Gelfand, "Yemen seeks assistance but rejects intervention," *JDW*, Vol. 47, No. 5, February 3, 2010; "Whitehall strengthens [Somali President] Sharif [Sheikh Ahmed]," *Africa Confidential*, Vol. 51, No. 6, March 19, 2010; Giles Whittel, "Silent war on militants to be extended with drones," *The Times*, August 27, 2010.

115. GEN129(73)first meeting, October 2, 1972; and GEN129(72)6, CAB130/616(NAUK); Minute by D. Stephen (MOD), March 13, 1973, DEFE25/282(NAUK); 22SAS refers to its constituent Companies as Squadrons, and its platoons as troops.

116. *Icon* involved a simulated hijacking at Stansted airport, and was used to test COBRA's operating procedures. GEN129(73) second meeting, July 3, 1973, CAB130/636(NAUK); Note by A. M. Goodenough, Maritime, Aviation, and Environment Department (FCO), October 24, 1977, FCO33/3186(NAUK).

117. Mark Bowden, *Guests of the Ayatollah*, London, UK: Atlantic Books, 2006, pp. 111-113; Naftali, *Blind Spot*, pp. 105-109.

118. 1977, FCO76/1755(NAUK).

119. John Parker, *SBS*, London, UK: Headline Press, 2004, pp. 282-283, 318; Tim Ripley, "Special Effects: UK SF unit comes into its own," *JDW*, Vol. 46, No. 8, February 25, 2009. Commachio Company was renamed the Fleet Protection Group in March 2001. See also *www.royalnavy.mod.uk/royalmarines/units-and-deployments/ other-royal-marine-units/fleet-protection-group-royal-marines/history/*.

120. Richard Clutterbuck, "Negotiating with Terrorists," and Alex Schmid, "Countering Terrorism in the Netherlands," in *Western Responses to Terrorism*, Schmid and Crelinstein, eds., pp. 84-85, 270-274.

121. Minute by Miss C. A. Lane, Home Office, *Inquest on the Five Iranian Terrorists*, February 4, 1981, HO299/110(NAUK). The hostage takers were ethnic Arabs from Southwestern Iran and were Iraqi-trained. Two diplomats were killed, one during the assault, the other, Abbas Lavasani (the press attaché), prior to this operation. Lavasani was shot dead by the terrorists in order to force the British government to accede to its demands. Instead, it led COBRA to authorize the Army to storm the embassy. "Anti-terror chief tells how siege gunmen died," *The Daily Telegraph*, May 10, 1980.

122. Wilkinson, *Terrorism versus Democracy*, p. 193; Lauren Gelfond Heldigger, "Back to Entebbe," *Jerusalem Post*, July 29, 2006; Martin van Crefeld, *The Sword and the Olive. A Critical History of the Israeli Defense Force*, New York: Public Affairs, 2002, p. 259. The Kenyan government facilitated the rescue mission by clandestinely granting the IDF over-flight rights.

123. General George Grivas-Dighenis, *Guerrilla Warfare and EOKA's Struggle: A Politico-Military Study*, A. A. Pallis, trans., London, UK: Longmans, 1964. Robert Thompson makes a similar point in *Defeating Communist Insurgency*, London, UK: Chatto & Windus, 1972, pp. 119-120, comparing the futility of sending a large dog to catch an alley cat, instead of using another cat to stealthily track down and confront its rival.

124. Hughes and Tripodi, "Surrogate," p. 6; Jonathan Walker, *Aden Insurgency. The Savage War in South Arabia*, Staplehurst, UK: Spellmount, 2005, pp. 184-185; IRN(74)2, Memorandum by Roy Mason, Defence Minister, *Army Plain Clothes Patrols in Northern Ireland*, March 28, 1974, CAB134/3778(NAUK).

125. James Rennie, *The Operators. Inside 14 Intelligence Company – The Army's Top Secret Elite*, London, UK: Century 1996; Mark Urban, *Big Boys' Rules: The Secret Struggle Against the IRA*, London, UK: Faber & Faber 1992, pp. 141-143; "Special forces regiment created," BBC News, April 5, 2005, available from *news.bbc.co.uk/1/hi/uk/4412907.stm*.

126. Rob Lewis, *Fishers of Men*, London, UK: Hodder & Stoughton, 1999; Martin Ingram and Greg Harkin, *Stakeknife. Britain's Secret Agents in Northern Ireland*, Dublin, Ireland: The O'Brien Press, 2004.

127. Ahron Bregman, *Israel's Wars. A History Since 1947*, London, UK: Routledge, 2nd Ed., 2004, pp. 220-224; Sergio Catignani, "The Israel Defense Forces and the *Al-Aqsa Intifada*: When Tactical Virtuosity Meets Strategic Disappointment," in Marston & Malkasian, *Counterinsurgency*, pp. 203-219.

128. Jeffrey Richelson, "'Truth Conquers All Chains': The U.S. Army's Intelligence Support Activity, 1981-1989," *International Journal of Intelligence and Counterintelligence*, Vol. 12, No. 2, 1999, pp. 168-200; Michael Smith, *Killer Elite*, London, UK: Cassell, 2006, pp. 31-46, 76-151.

129. James Bamford, *Body of Secrets: How America's NSA and Britain's GCHQ Spy on the World*, London, UK: Century, 2001; Michael Smith, *The Spying Game: The Secret History of British Espionage*, London, UK: Politico's, 2003, pp. 305-322. In addition to its headquarters at Fort Meade, Maryland, the NSA has a listening post at RAF Menwith Hill, Yorkshire, England. GCHQ is based in Cheltenham, Gloucestershire, England, and is also assisted by the Joint Service Signal Unit, a Royal Signals/RAF formation) based at Akrotiri, Cyprus, which provides a SIGINT interception capability for the Middle East. The British armed forces also contribute to intelligence gathering in the following fields: The Army's Intelligence Corps has a HUMINT role, while the RAF has tradi-

tionally operated as a gatherer of IMINT (Imagery Intelligence). Major General Graham Messervy-Whiting, "British armed forces and European Union perspectives on countering terrorism," in Siniver, *International Terrorism*, p. 101.

130. "Echelon: Big brother with a cause?" BBC News, July 6, 2002, available from *news.bbc.co.uk/1/hi/world/europe/820758.stm*; Bamford, *Body of Secrets*, pp. 394-403, 410.

131. Ken Connor, *Ghost Force: The Secret History of the SAS*, London, UK: Weidenfeld & Nicholson, 1998, p. 190; Taylor, *Brits*, pp. 270-277.

132. Urban, *Big Boys' Rules*, pp. 220-237; Toby Harnden, *Bandit Country: The IRA and South Armagh*, London, UK: Hodder & Stoughton 1999, pp. 418-423; Van der Bijl, *Operation Banner*, pp. 174-175, 180, 193.

133. Taylor, *Brits*, pp. 1, 302; Bradley Bamford, "The Role and Effectiveness of Intelligence in Northern Ireland," *Intelligence and National Security*, Vol. 20, No. 4, 2005, pp. 592-593; Peter R. Neumann, *Britain's Longest War. British Strategy in the Northern Ireland Conflict, 1969-98*, Basingstoke, England: Palgrave, 2003, p. 157; Moloney, *IRA*, pp. 304-319.

134. Deborah Haynes, "General Petraeus hails SAS after Iraq success over al-Qaeda car bombers," *The Times*, August 11, 2008; Speech by John Hutton, available from *www.acronym.org/docs/0904/doc13.htm*; Mark Urban, *Task Force Black*, New York: Little, Brown, 2010.

135. Cronin, *How Terrorism Ends*, pp. 24-25; Major General Julian Thompson, *War Behind Enemy Lines*, New York: Macmillan, 1999, pp. 52-55; Peter Calvocoressi, Guy Wint, and John Pritchard, *Total War: The Causes and Courses of World War Two: Volume II: The Greater East Asia and Pacific Conflict*, London, UK: Penguin, 1989, pp. 494-495.

136. Williamson Murray, and Major General Robert Scales, Jr., *The Iraq War: A Military History*, Cambridge MA: Harvard University Press, 2004, pp. 150-151, 154-156; Patrick Cockburn, "Chemical Ali: The end of an overlord," *The Independent*, June 25, 2007.

137. Trefor Moss, "U.S. strike kills al-Qaeda leaders in Pakistan," *JDW*, Vol. 46, No. 2, January 14, 2009; Daniel Markey, *Securing Pakistan's Tribal Belt*, Special Report No. 36, Washington, DC: Council on Foreign Relations, August 2008, pp. 18-19.

138. Frank Gardner, *Blood and Sand*, London, UK: Bantam Press, 2007, pp. 280-281; Tristan McConnell, "Terrorist Saleh Ali Saleh Nabhan killed by U.S. commandos in Somalia," *The Times*, September 16, 2009. Nabhan is accused of complicity in the Mombasa bomb attacks of October 2002.

139. Patrick Porter, "Long wars and long telegrams: containing Al-Qaeda," *International Affairs*, Vol. 85, No. 2, 2009, p. 301; Omar Waraich, "'Shoot-out' at Taliban meeting," *The Independent*, August 10, 2009; Saeed Shah, "Pakistani Taliban Appoints Fearsome Young Gun as New Leader," *The Daily Telegraph*, August 24, 2009.

140. Joby Warrick and Peter Finn, "Al-Qaeda is a Wounded and Dangerous Enemy," *Washington Post*, February 8, 2010; Peter Taylor, "The wannabe British jihadist who said no to Al-Qaeda," *The Times*, February 21, 2010.

141. *Mossad*'s operations include the killing of Mahmoud al-Mabhouh, a senior Hamas military commander, in Dubai on January 20, 2010. Alon Ben David, "Spy games: Mossad returns to form," *JIR*, Vol. 22, No. 5, 2010, pp. 26-31.

142. Simon Reeve, *One Day in September*, London, UK: Faber & Faber, 2000, pp. 160-188; Said Aburish, *Arafat; From Defender to Dictator*, New York: Bloomsbury 1998, pp. 203-210; James Corum and Wray Johnson, *Airpower in Small Wars; Fighting Insurgents and Terrorists*, Lawrence: University Press of Kansas, 2003, p. 414.

143. Lisa Beyer, Ron Ben-Yishai, and Jamil Hamad, "Deadly Force," *Time Magazine*, August 24, 1992; Clive Jones, "'One Size Fits All': Israel, Intelligence and the *al-Aqsa Intifada*," *SC&T*, Vol. 26, No. 4, 2003, pp. 273-275; *The Dirty War: Israel Undercover*, documentary broadcast on BBC2, February 17, 2002.

144. Robert Pape, *Bombing to Win; Airpower and Coercion in War*, Ithaca, NY: Cornell University Press, 1996, pp. 12-13.

145. Yezid Sayigh, *Armed Struggle and the Search for State: The Palestinian National Movement, 1949-1993,* OUP, 1999, pp. 62-65, 124, 176-179; Barry Rubin, *Revolution until Victory? The History and Politics of the PLO,* Cambridge, MA: Harvard University Press, 1994, pp. 139-141.

146. Joseph T. Stanik, *El Dorado Canyon: Reagan's Undeclared War Against Gaddafi,* Annapolis, MD: Naval Institute Press, 2003.

147. Damla Aras, "The Role of Motivation in the Success of Coercive Diplomacy: The 1998 Turkish-Syrian Crisis as a Case Study," *Defence Studies,* Vol. 9, No. 2, 2009, pp. 207-223.

148. Robert Fisk, *Pity the Nation; Lebanon at War,* OUP, 1992, pp. 524-525; Edgar O'Ballance, *Civil War in Lebanon, 1975-92,* Basingstoke, England: Macmillan, 1998, p. 133.

149. Richard A. Clarke, *Against All Enemies; Inside America's War on Terror,* London, UK: Free Press, 2004, pp. 184-187; Steve Coll, *Ghost Wars; The Secret History of the CIA, Afghanistan and bin Laden, from the Soviet Invasion to September 10th, 2001,* London, UK: Penguin, 2005, pp. 416-431.

150. Tatiana Waisberg, "The Colombia-Ecuador Armed Crisis of March, 2008: The Practice of Targeted Killing and Incursions against Non-State Actors Harbored at Terrorist Safe Havens in a Third Party State," *SC&T,* Vol. 32, No. 6, 2009, pp. 476-488.

151. Bregman, *Israel's Wars,* pp. 158-176; Bergman, *Secret War,* pp. 364-377; Alon Ben-David, "Israeli offensive seeks 'new security reality' in Gaza"; and Mohammed Najib, "Hamas is 'on the defensive' in Gaza crisis," *JDW,* Vol. 46, No. 2, January 14, 2009.

152. Byman, *Deadly Connections,* pp. 209-210; Rohan Gunaratna, *Inside Al Qaeda,* New York: Berkley Press, 2003, pp. 78-80.

153. William Maley, *The Afghanistan Wars,* Basingstoke, England: Palgrave, 2002, pp. 262-268; Anthony Davis, "How the Afghan war was won," *JIR,* Vol. 14, No. 2, 2002, pp. 6-13.

154. Sayigh, *Armed Struggle,* pp. 509-510; Stephen Biddle, "Allies, Airpower, and Modern Warfare: The Afghan Model in Af-

ghanistan and Iraq," *International Security*, Vol. 30, No. 3, 2005-06, pp. 161-176; Alistair Finlan, *Special Forces, Strategy and the War on Terror*, London, UK: Routledge, 2008, pp. 111-138.

155. Peter John Paul Krause, "The Last Good Chance: A Reassessment of U.S. Operations at Tora Bora," *Security Studies*, Vol. 17, No. 4, 2008, pp. 644-684; Benjamin Lambeth, *Air Power against Terror: America's Conduct of Operation Enduring Freedom*, Santa Monica CA: RAND Corporation, 2005, pp. 149-154.

156. Edmund Sanders and Abukar Albadri, "Renewed Fighting Edges Somalia Closer to Civil War," *Chicago Tribune*, December 21, 2006; Lauren Gelfand, "Ethiopia starts withdrawal of troops from Somalia," *JDW*, Vol. 46, No. 2, January 14, 2009; "Good-bye, maybe," *Africa Confidential*, Vol. 50, No. 3, February 6, 2009; "Al-Qaeda on the March," *The Economist*, May 22, 2009.

157. Andrew, *Defence of the Realm*, p. 741; One CIA officer explaining the lack of his Agency's attention to Afghanistan prior to 9/11 — and its inability to send operatives to monitor the emergence of al-Qaeda during the late 1990s — wryly noted that "[operations] that include diarrhoea as a way of life simply don't happen," and that the majority of CIA officers were loath to experience the danger and discomfort involved in operating clandestinely in Taliban-ruled Afghanistan. Steve Hewitt, "American Counter-terrorism through the Rewards for Justice Program, 1984-2008," in Siniver, *International Terrorism*, p. 85.

158. "Iraq legacy for Afghan campaign," BBC News, September 26, 2009, available from *news.bbc.co.uk/1/hi/programmes/from_our_own_correspondent/8274993.stm*. Stephen Gray discusses the British Army's attitude in "Cracking on in Helmand," *Prospect Magazine*, Vol. 162, August 27, 2009.

159. Declan Walsh, "U.S. soldiers and teenage girls killed in bombing near Pakistan school," *The Guardian*, February 3, 2010.

160. "Front Line Vets," *The Economist*, January 30, 2010; Vogl, "Train to Gain?"

161. Ben Rawlence, "Trained in Terror," July 30, 2008, available from *www.guardian.co.uk/commentisfree/2008/jul/30/Kenya.Terrorism/print*.

162. Daniel Byman, "Friends Like These: Counterinsurgency and the War on Terrorism," *International Security*, Vol. 31, No. 2, 2006, pp. 79-115.

163. Hilary Synnott, *Transforming Pakistan: Ways out of Instability*, Adelphi Paper No. 406, 2009, p. 123; Alistair Harris and Michael Page, "The State of Yemen," *RUSI Journal*, Vol. 154, No. 6, 2009, pp. 68-72.

164. Abdul Hameed Bakier, "Jihadis Discuss Plans to Seize Pakistan's Nuclear Arsenal," *JFTM*, Vol. 7, No. 14, May 26, 2009.

165. Craig Murray, *Murder in Samarkand*, Edinburgh, Scotland: Mainstream Publishing, 2006; "Last U.S. plane leaves Uzbek base," BBC News, November 21, 2005, available from *news.bbc. co.uk, No. 1, No. hi/world/asia-pacific/4457844.stm*.

166. Roger McDermott, "Uzbekistan Playing Renewed Strategic Role in NATO's Afghanistan Mission," *Jamestown Eurasia Daily Monitor*, Vol. 6, No. 38, February 26, 2009; Joshua Kucera, "U.S. seeks rapprochement with Uzbekistan," *JDW*, Vol. 47, No. 1, January 6, 2010.

167. Anthony Loyd, "Short of kit, short of support: How the British Army failed in Basra," *The Times*, March 18, 2008; Hala Jaber, "We will spill British blood, warns Sheikh Ahmad Fartusi," *The Sunday Times*, September 14, 2008. Sheikh Fartusi was the commander of the Mahdi Army in Basra.

168. Tariq Mahmud Ashraf, "Taming the ISI: Implications for Pakistan's Stability and the War on Terrorism," *JFTM*, Vol. 6, No. 20, October 24, 2008; Shuja Nawaz, *Crossed Swords: Pakistan, its Army, and the Wars Within*, OUP, 2008, pp. 438-440, 467-469, 545.

169. Tariq Mahmud Ashraf, "The Pakistan Frontier Corps in the War on Terrorism," Part I in *JFTM*, Vol. 6, No. 15, July 25, 2008; Part II in *JFTM*, Vol. 6, No. 16, August 11, 2008.

170. Paul Dixon, ""Hearts and Minds'? British Counter-Insurgency from Malaya to Iraq," *The Journal of Strategic Studies*, Vol. 32, No. 3, 2009, p. 360; William Rosenau, *U.S. Internal Assistance to South Vietnam: Insurgency, Subversion and Public Order*, London, UK: Routledge, 2005, pp. 90-91, 97-100.

171. Lawrence Freedman, *A Choice of Enemies: America Confronts the Middle East*, London, UK: Phoenix, 2009, pp. 170-171.

172. J. N. Dixit, *India-Pakistan in War and Peace, London, UK: Routledge,* 2002, pp. 23-25. One of the freed militants, Omar Saeed Sheikh, was subsequently sentenced to death for the kidnapping and murder of *Wall Street Journal* reporter Daniel Pearl. "Profile: Omar Saeed Sheikh," BBC News, July 16, 2002, available from *news.bbc.co.uk/1/hi/uk/1804710.stm*.

173. Bowden, *Guests of the Ayatollah*, p. 138, 223-233, 431-468. See also the report commissioned by the Joint Chiefs of Staff, produced by a panel headed by Admiral James L. Holloway (USN), August 23, 1980, available from *www.gwu.edu/~nsarchiv/NSAEBB/ NSAEBB63/doc8.pdf*. An invasion of Iran would have outraged regional opinion, alarmed U.S. NATO allies, and could possibly have provoked a major crisis with the USSR.

174. The *Sayeret Maktal* killed two out of the four PFLP hijackers in the operation; three passengers were wounded, with one succumbing to her injuries. "1972: Israeli commandos storm hijacked jet," available from *news.bbc.co.uk/onthisday/hi/dates/stories/ may/9/newsid_4326000/4326706.htm*; Reeve, *One Day in September*, p. 75; James Adams, *Secret Armies*, London, UK: Hutchinson 1988, pp. 89-95.

175. Jeffrey Goldberg, 'The Point of No Return," *The Atlantic Monthly*, September 2010.

176. Naftali, *Blind Spot*, pp. 130-135, 142-143; The United States did subsequently launch air strikes against Syrian military and Druze militia targets in December 1983. See Freedman, *Choice of Enemies*, p. 144; Richard Lock-Pullan, *U.S. Intervention Policy and Army Innovation: From Vietnam to Iraq*, London, UK: Routledge, 2006.

177. For the current debate within the U.S. Army, see Lieutenant Colonel John Nagl, "Let's Win the Wars We're In," and Colonel Gian Gentile, "Let's Build an Army to Win all Wars," *Joint Force Quarterly*, Vol. 52, No. 1, 2009, pp. 20-33.

178. Benjamin and Simon, *Sacred Terror*, pp. 294-295; *The National Commission on Terrorist Attacks Upon the United States: The 9/11 Report*, New York: St Martin's Press, 2004, pp. 190-191, 196-199.

179. Richard Scott, "ASW Resurfaces," *JDW*, Vol. 45, No. 24, June 11, 2008; Comments by General Sir Richard Dannatt (GCS) at the Royal United Services Institute Future Land War Conference, June 18, 2008, p. 8, available from *www.rusi.org/downloads/assets/Dannatspeech2008.pdf*.

180. Jason Burke, *Al-Qaeda*, London, UK: Penguin, 2007, pp. 180-182; Gunaratna, *Inside Al Qaeda*, pp. 63-64; Benjamin and Simon, *Sacred Terror*, p. 153; "Punish and be damned," *The Economist*, August 29, 1998.

181. The question came from Graydon Carter of *Vanity Fair*; Benjamin and Simon, *Sacred Terror*, p. 261; Clarke, *Against All Enemies*, p. 186.

182. Clarke, *Against All Enemies*, p. 190.

183. Jane Corbin, *The Base*, London, UK: Simon & Schuster, 2003, pp. 299-308.

184. "Hezbollah Leader: Militants 'Won't Surrender Arms'," CNN News, September 22, 2006, available from *edition.cnn.com/2006/WORLD/meast/09/22/Lebanon.rally/*.

185. Christopher Andrew, *For the President's Eyes Only: Secret Intelligence and the American Presidency from Washington to Bush*, New York: HarperCollins, 1995, pp. 483-484; Wilkinson, *Terrorism Versus Democracy*, p. 129.

186. Michael Walzer, *Just and Unjust Wars*, New York: Basic Books 1992, pp. 51-73; Waisberg, "Colombia-Ecuador Crisis," p. 479. The resolutions referred to here are available from *www.un.org/Docs/sc/unsc_resolutions.html*.

187. Benjamin and Simon, *Sacred Terror*, pp. 273-275, 315; Rashid, *Descent into Chaos*, pp. 72-73, 77-78.

188. See Paddy Ashdown, "What We Must Do to Win this War in Afghanistan," *The Independent*, July 22, 2009.

189. "Israel and Sri Lanka: A Media Analysis of War Crimes Investigations," report by *Just Journalism*, June 2009, available

from *www.justjournalism.com/special-reports/view/israel-and-sri-lan-ka-a-media-analysis-of-war-crimes-allegations*; Clancy Chassay and Julian Borger, "Guardian Investigation Uncovers Evidence of Alleged Israeli War Crimes in Gaza," *The Guardian*, March 24, 2009; Catherine Philp, "The hidden massacre: Sri Lanka's final offensive against the Tamil Tigers," *The Times*, May 29, 2009.

190. "Israel debates response to Gaza report," BBC News, October 24, 2009, available from *news.bbc.co.uk/1/hi/world/middle_east/8322584.stm*. The Goldstone report is available from *www2. ohchr.org/english/bodies/hrcouncil/specialsession/9/docs/UNFFMGC_Report.pdf*.

191. Interview with Noam Chomsky by Suzy Hansen on *Salon.com*, January 16, 2002, available from *www.chomsky.info/interviews/20020116.htm*. See comments by Carol Bogert, the HRW Communications Director, on January 22, 2002, available from *dir.salon.com/story/people/leters/2002/01/22/chomsky/index.html*. Werner Daum, the German ambassador to Sudan between 1996-2000, offered a retrospective guess that "several tens of thousands of Sudanese may have died as a result of the destruction of the al-Shifa factory in 'Universalism and the West'," *Harvard International Review*, Vol. 23, No. 2, 2001, available from *www.harvardir. org/index.php?page=article&id=909&p=*. As far as Chomsky's methodology is concerned, this constitutes an official report endorsed by the German government.

192. Robert Fisk publicized the massacre claims in "The Credibility of U.S. Policy on the Conflict Has Been Shattered," *Independent on Sunday*, April 14, 2002. HRW was critical of the IDF's tactics but cited 52 Palestinian dead, 22 of whom were civilians, thereby denying Palestinian claims (reported uncritically by Fisk and other media sources) that hundreds of civilians had been deliberately slaughtered by the Israelis; "'No Jenin massacre' say rights group," BBC News, May 3, 2002, available from *news.bbc. co.uk/1/hi/world/middle_east/1965471.stm*. See also Peter Beaumont, "Not a Massacre, but a Brutal Breach of War's Rules," *The Guardian*, April 25, 2002.

193. Benjamin and Simon, *Sacred Terror*, p. 260; Paul R. Pillar, *Terrorism and U.S. Foreign Policy*, Washington, DC: Brookings, 2001, p. 108. The CIA acquired a soil sample from the site that showed traces of the chemical EMPTA, which is created during

the production of a highly lethal nerve agent known as VX. Nerve agents kill through contact with the skin, and consist of persistent agents (notably liquid weapons such as VX) and non-persistent agents (which includes the Sarin gas which Aum Shinrikyo used in the Tokyo subway attack of 1995).

194. Adam Roberts, "Ethics, Terrorism and Counter-Terrorism," *Terrorism and Political Violence*, Vol. 1, No. 1, 1989, p. 60; David C. Gompert, "Underkill: Fighting Extremists amid Populations," *Survival*, Vol. 51, No. 2, 2009, pp. 159-160.

195. For contrasting views, see "Statement by Professor Richard Falk, UN Special Rapporteur for Human Rights in the Occupied Territories," December 27, 2008, available from *www.unhchr. ch/huricane/huricane.nsf/view01/F1EC67EF7A498A30C125752D005 D17F7?opendocument*. See also Anthony Cordesman, "The "Gaza War": A Strategic Analysis," Washington, DC: Center for Strategic and International Studies, February 2, 2009, available from *csis.org/files/media/csis/pubs/090202_gaza_war.pdf*.

196. Ethan Bronner, "Hamas shifts from rockets to culture war," *New York Times*, July 24, 2009; Amos Harel and Avi Issacharoff, "A New Kind of War," *Foreign Policy*, January 20, 2010, available from *www.foreignpolicy.com/articles/2010/01/20/a_new_kind_of_war*; Yaakov Katz and Herb Keinon, "Hamas Rockets Seen as Bid to Foil Talks," August 2, 2010.

197. *9/11 Report*, pp. 191-203; Coll, *Ghost Wars*, pp. 445-447. Alongside Pakistan and Saudi Arabia, the UAE was the only country to recognize the Taliban regime prior to 9/11. As odd as it may seem to Western readers, wealthy Gulf Arabs often visited Taliban-ruled Afghanistan to indulge in one of their favorite pastimes, hunting with falcons.

198. Naftali, *Blind Spot*, p. 248. For a partial account based on the then-FBI Director's recollections, see Elsa Walsh, "Louis Freeh's Last Case," *The New Yorker*, May 14, 2001.

199. Gardner, *Blood and Sand*, pp. 280-281; Hilary Synnott, "What is Happening in Pakistan?" *Survival*, Vol. 51, No. 1, 2009, pp. 65-71; Pantucci, "Deep Impact," p. 74.

200. Synnott, *Transforming Pakistan*, pp. 12, 161; Brian Clough-ley, "Uneasy partnership. The U.S. and Pakistan's dysfunctional alliance," *JIR*, Vol. 22, No. 5, 2010, pp. 8-13.

201. "Nigerian doubts over AFRICOM base," BBC News, November 20, 2007, available from *news.bbc.co.uk/1,/hi/world/ africa/7104215.stm*; Laurie Nathan, "AFRICOM: A Threat to Af-rica's Security," *Contemporary Security Policy*, Vol. 30, No. 1, 2009, pp. 58-61. For a rebuttal, see Vice-Admiral Robert Moeller (U.S. Navy), "The Truth about AFRICOM," *Foreign Policy*, July 21, 2010.

202. Vogl, "Train to Gain?"; "AFRICOM's Operation *Flintlock*: New Partners and New Questions," *JFTM*, Vol. 8, No. 22, June 5, 2010.

203. Michael D. Milalka and Lieutenant Colonel Mark R. Wil-cox, "Unintended Consequences of Security Assistance in the South Caucasus," *Joint Force Quarterly*, Vol. 57, No. 2, 2010, pp. 25-32.

204. GEN(76)1st meeting, *Cabinet Committee on Northern Ire-land*, May 24, 1976, CAB130, No. 908(NAUK); J. Stewart, Northern Ireland Office (NIO) to P. Wright, 10 Downing Street, August 24, 1976, PREM16, No. 1342(NAUK); Tony Geraghty, *The Irish War*, London, UK: HarperCollins 1998, p. 223.

205. Urban, *Big Boys' Rules*, p. 10; Hamill, *Pig in the Middle*, pp. 162. MOD files refer to Anglo-Irish police and military coop-eration as far back as 1973. Lieutenant Colonel D. Ramsbotham, *Visit by CGS to Northern Ireland*, September 28, 1973, DEFE13, No. 990(NAUK); Van der Bijl, *Operation Banner*, pp. 83, 88.

206. Bill Park, *Turkey's Policy Towards Northern Iraq: Problems and Perspectives*, Adelphi Paper No. 374, 2005, pp. 56-61; "Turkish troops enter Northern Iraq," BBC News, February 22, 2008, avail-able from *news.bbc.co.uk/1/hi/world/europe/7258323.stm*.

207. Bregman, *Israel's Wars*, pp. 147-148; Ahron Bregman and Jihan el-Tahri, *The Fifty Years War: Israel and the Arabs*, London, UK: Penguin, 1998, pp. 156-157; Freedman, *Choice of Enemies*, pp. 126-135.

208. Candace Rondeaux and Karen DeYoung, "U.S. Troops Crossed Border, Pakistan says," *Washington Post*, September 4, 2008; Pantucci, "Deep Impact," p. 73; "Front Line Against the Taliban," *The Economist*, November 26, 2009.

209. Pantucci, "Deep Impact," p. 73; "Mapping U.S. drone and Islamic militant attacks in Pakistan," BBC News, July 22, 2010, available from *www.bbc.co.uk/news/world-south-asia-10648909*.

210. Dave Sloggett, "Attack of the drones: The utility of UAVs in fighting terrorism," *JIR*, Vol. 22, No. 8, 2010, pp. 14-18; Farhat Taj, "Drone attacks: Pakistan's Policy and the Tribesmen's Perspective," *JTSM*, Vol. 23, No. 10, March 11, 2010; Tom Baldwin, "Concern mounts over US *Predator* covert killings," *The Times*, May 23, 2009.

211. Cronin, *How Terrorism Ends*, p. 15; and *Ending Terrorism*, p. 32; Mette Eilstrup-Sangiovanni and Calvert Jones, "Assessing the Dangers of Illicit Networks: Why al-Qaeda May Be Less Threatening Than Many Think," *International Security*, Vol. 33, No. 2, 2008, pp. 21-23.

212. Tracey German, "David and Goliath: Georgia and Russia's Coercive Diplomacy," *Defence Studies*, Vol. 9, No. 2, 2009, pp. 230-231.

213. Bob Woodward, *Plan of Attack*, London, UK: Simon & Schuster, 2004, pp. 24-27; Bergman, *Secret War*, p. 56; Crefeld, *Sword and Olive*, pp. 285-306.

214. Andrew Cockburn and Patrick Cockburn, *Saddam Hussein: An American Obsession*, London, UK: Verso, 2002, p. 165; Con Coughlin, *Saddam: The Secret Life*, Macmillan, 2002, pp. 140-145; Byman, *Deadly Connections*, pp. 292-294.

215. Sayigh, *Armed Struggle*, pp. 61-66; Keith Kyle, *Suez*, London, UK: I. B. Tauris, 2003, pp. 55-60, 107, 301, 315, 347; Michael Oren, *Six Days of War*, London, UK: Penguin, 2003, pp. 34-35.

216. Owen Bennett Jones, *Pakistan: Eye of the Storm*, New Haven, CT: Yale University Press, 2002, pp. 209-210.

217. Victoria Schofield, *Kashmir in Conflict: India, Pakistan and the Unending War*, London, UK: I. B.Tauris, 2003, p. 235; Srinath Raghavan, "A Coercive Triangle: India, Pakistan, the United States, and the Crisis of 2001-2001," *Defence Studies*, Vol. 9, No. 2, 2009, pp. 244-258.

218. Rabasa *et al*, *Mumbai*, p. 16. U.S. Secretary of Defense Robert Gates has suggested that provoking an Indo-Pakistani war might be an al-Qaeda objective. "Gates Warns of Militants in South Asia," *Wall Street Journal*, January 21, 2010.

219. Chin, "War on Terror," pp. 130, 135-136. Hassan Butt refutes this impression in "My Plea to Fellow Muslims: You Must Renounce Terror," *The Observer*, July 1, 2007. An ex-Islamist militant, Butt states that radical Islamism is only superficially motivated by grievances such as Iraq, and that its main motivation is "[to fight] for the creation of a revolutionary state that would eventually bring Islamic justice to the world." To offer some confirmation for Butt's argument, a recent report by the House of Commons Intelligence and Security Committee notes that Siddique Khan, the 7/7 ringleader, was present at a militant training camp in 2001 prior to the Afghanistan and Iraq wars. See CM7617, *Could 7/7 Have Been Prevented? Review of the Intelligence on the London Terrorist Attacks on 7 July, 2005*, London, UK: The Stationery Office, 2009, p. 14.

220. Kim Sengupta, "Afghan War Tied to Security at Home," *The Independent*, August 3, 2009; Bergman, *Secret War*, pp. 251-252.

221. S. E. Finer, *The Man on Horseback; The Role of the Military in Politics*, London, UK: Penguin, 1976, pp. 219-222; Michael Howard, *War and the Liberal Conscience*, London, UK: Temple Smith, 1978, pp. 76-78, 129, 133-135; Charles Townshend, *Britain's Civil Wars: Counterinsurgency in the Twentieth Century*, London, UK: Faber & Faber, 1986, pp. 15-23.

222. For an analysis of civil-military discord from a UK perspective, see Hew Strachan, *The Politics of the British Army*, Oxford, UK: Clarendon Press, 1997; and "Making Strategy," pp. 59-82.

223. "Questions on CCRF answered by Lord Bach, Parliamentary Under-Secretary of State (MOD), October 28, 2004," Parlia-

mentary Debates Lords, available from *www.publications.parlia-ment.uk/pa/ld200304/ldhansrd/vo041028/text/41028-03.htm*; SDR *New Chapter.*

224. Neil Tweedie, "Cash and Manpower Shortages Leave Emergency Military Force 'in Chaos'," *Daily Telegraph*, September 12, 2005. The MOD's website is bereft of references to the CCRF. The author participated in two London District CCRF practice mobilizations in February and November 2003, both of which could best be described as a shambles. The November 2003 exercise involved a CBRN attack, and it became clear that the Royal Navy reservists participating in this scenario had no Nuclear, Biological and Chemical (NBC) defense training whatsoever. An Army captain serving in the London District Training Team had to provide an impromptu lesson on how to wear their NBC suits, don respirators, and decontaminate themselves. Aside from two exercises conducted by London District in 2006 and 2007, the author could find no further reference to any other CCRF activity.

225. Patrick Barkham, "Heathrow show of force after terror alert," *The Times*, February 12, 2003. An example of the widespread skepticism felt over the 2003 alert can be seen in the *Guardian*'s editorial cartoon on February 13, 2003, available from *www.guardian.co.uk/cartoons/stevebell/0,7371,894734,00.html*.

226. Stephen Dorril and Robin Ramsay, *Smear: Wilson and the Secret State*, New York: HarperCollins, 1992, p. 268; Strachan, *Politics of the British Army*, pp. 187-189.

227. Roger Faligot, *Britain's Military Strategy in Ireland: The Kitson Experiment*, London, UK: Zed Books, 1983; Paul Foot, *Who Framed Colin Wallace?* London, UK: Macmillan, 1989; Paul-Marie de la Gorce, Kenneth Douglas, trans., *The French Army: A Military-Political History*, London, UK: Weidenfeld and Nicholson, 1963, pp. 531-552.

228. Roberts, "Terrorism and Counter-Terrorism," p. 60.

229. Rod Thornton, "Getting it Wrong: The Crucial Mistakes made in the Early Stages of the British Army's Deployment in Northern Ireland, August 1969 to March 1972," *Journal of Strategic Studies*, Vol. 30, No. 1, 2007, pp. 76-79.

230. Thornton, "Getting it Wrong," p. 76; *Meeting between the Defence Secretary and the Northern Ireland Government at Stormont*, March 20, 1971, DEFE25/304(NAUK).

231. Background note, *Relations between the Army and the RUC*, July 29, 1970, DEFE24/980(NAUK); Hennessey, *Troubles*, pp. 13, 16-18. Despite a constant effort by the British authorities after 1970 to create a neutral, bisectarian force, only 8 percent of the RUC consisted of Catholics by 1997. "New Cop in Town," *The Economist*, November 5, 2009.

232. Hamill, *Pig in the Middle*, pp. 221-227, 231-233, 252; Tuck, "Northern Ireland," pp. 169-170.

233. GEN129(73)6, *Contingency Plans*, February 19, 1973; GEN129(73)1st meeting, February 23, 1973, CAB130, No. 636(NAUK); General Sir Peter de la Billiere, *Looking for Trouble*, London, UK: HarperCollins 1995, pp. 280-283.

234. "Protection of Offshore Installations," note on an inter-departmental meeting held September 25, 1974; DP18/74(Final), *The Responsibilities of the Armed Forces for Safeguarding the United Kingdom's Offshore Interests in Peace*, October 18, 1974, DEFE24, No. 411(NAUK).

235. Memorandum by A. S. Baker (Home Office), March 25, 1977, FCO76/1755(NAUK); Duncan Falconer, *First Into Action: A Dramatic Personal Account of Life in the SBS*, London, UK: Sphere, 2001, p. 322.

236. Rabasa *et al*, *Mumbai*, pp. 10-11; "India's security — learning from Mumbai," BBC News, November 11, 2009, available from *news.bbc.co.uk/1/hi/world/south_asia/8373836.stm*.

237. Sean O'Neill, "Cobra emergency committee 'slows everything down'," *The Times*, June 22, 2009.

238. General Frank Kitson, *Low Intensity Operations*, 2nd Ed., London, UK: Faber & Faber 1991, pp. 95-96. Kitson served with the British Army in the Kenyan and Malayan campaigns, and was Commanding Officer, 39th Brigade (Belfast), during the early 1970s. The importance of intelligence is also emphasized by the U.S. and British Army COIN manuals; FM 3-24, p. 3.1; AFM1 10, pp. B-6-1 - B-6-18.

239. One of *Shin Bet*'s agents was Mosab Hassan Yousef, the son of Hamas's co-founder Sheikh Hassan Yousef. James Hider, "Son of Hamas founder spied for Israel to stop bombers," *The Times*, February 25, 2010.

240. Hughes and Tripodi, "Surrogate," pp. 8-9; Lawrence Freedman, *The Transformation of Strategic Affairs*, Adelphi Paper No. 379, 2006, pp. 90-91; Naftali, *Blind Spot*, pp. 198-199.

241. Bergman, *Secret War*, pp. 76-81; Walker, *Aden Insurgency*, pp. 184-185, 191.

242. Minute by Deputy Chief of Defence Staff (Intelligence), December 21, 1972, DEFE25/282(NAUK); Field Marshal Michael Carver, *Out of Step*, London, UK: Hutchinson, 1989, p. 429; Lieutenant Colonel J. Biles, *Chief of the General Staff's Visit to Northern Ireland, Wednesday, 5 Feb 1975*, February 6, 1975, DEFE11/917(NAUK).

243. Urban, *Big Boys' Rules*, pp. 20-23, 109-110; Ramsbotham minute, September 28, 1973, DEFE13/990(NAUK); Bamford, "Intelligence," pp. 593-594; Moloney, *IRA*, pp. 332-33, 335-336, 458-459.

244. Dillon, *Dirty War*, pp. 29-45; Jaber, "We will spill British blood," *The Sunday Times*.

245. For descriptions of these crises and the civilian casualties, see Carlotta Gall and Thomas de Waal, *Chechnya; A Small Victorious War*, London, UK: Macmillan, 1997, pp. 256-275, 290-304; Robert Saunders, "A Conjurer's Game: Vladimir Putin and the Politics of Presidential Prestidigitation," in Kassimeris, ed., *Playing Politics*, pp. 220-249.

246. Bennett, *Crying Wolf*, pp. 428-435; Anatol Lieven, *Chechnya: Tombstone of Russian Power*, New Haven, CT: Yale University Press 1998, pp. 124-125, 138-139.

247. Kramer, "Chechnya," p. 54; Saunders, "A Conjurer's Game," pp. 234-240; "Russia: Independent Beslan Investigation Sparks Controversy," RFE, No. RL report, August 29, 2006, available from *www.rferl.org/content/article,/1070905.html*.

248. Paul Wallace, "Political Violence and Terrorism in India: The Crisis of Identity," in Martha Crenshaw, ed., *Terrorism in Context*, University Park, PA: Pennsylvania State University Press, 1995, pp. 385-386.

249. Minute by Ian Gilmour, Under-Secretary of State for Army, *The Shooting of Daniel O'Hagan, 31 July 1970*, September 3, 1970, DEFE24/980(NAUK). The author's experiences of public order training have left him with the sincere wish that he never witnesses a genuine riot.

250. Hennessey, *Troubles*, pp. 250-253, 257-263; Thornton, "Getting it Wrong," p. 99.

251. Hennessey, *Troubles*, p. 348. Other subunits of 1PARA in Londonderry that day (not to mention soldiers from other battalions) held their fire during the demonstration and the ensuing rioting. The Saville Inquiry presented its conclusions on "Bloody Sunday" on June 15, 2010. Its findings blamed soldiers from Support Company, 1 PARA, for "unjustifiable firing," and implicitly repudiated an earlier inquiry by Lord Widgery (April 1972) by stressing that the demonstrators were unarmed, available from *report.bloody-sunday-inquiry.org* .

252. Michael Dewar, *The British Army in Northern Ireland*, London, UK: Arms and Armour Press 1997, p. 38.

253. Quoted in Schofield, *Kashmir*, p. 168. See pp. 168-170, on Indian military and security force abuses during the 1990s.

254. Jane Perlez and Pir Zubair Shah, "Pakistan Army is Said to be Linked to Many Killings in Swat," *New York Times*, September 15, 2009; "The Law in Whose Hands?" *The Economist*, October 3, 2009.

255. Neumann, "The Myth of Ulsterization"; Van der Bijl, *Operation Banner*, p. 31.

256. Paul Dixon, "'Hearts and Minds'? British Counter-Insurgency Strategy in Northern Ireland," *Journal of Strategic Studies*, Vol. 32, No. 2, 2009, p. 467; Martin Dillon, *The Dirty War*, London, UK: Arrow Books, 1990, pp. 211-230; Tony Geraghty, *The*

Irish War, New York: HarperCollins 1998, p. 229; Hamill, *Pig in the Middle*, pp. 299-305; Following the 1991 Defence Review, the UDR was incorporated into the regular army as the Home Service Battalions of the Royal Irish Regiment.

257. Donatella Della Porta, "Institutional Response to Terrorism: The Italian Case," in Crelinstein and Schmid, *Western Responses to Terrorism*, pp. 153-154; John Dickie refers to *dietrologia* in a different context in *Cosa Nostra; A History of the Sicilian Mafia*, London, UK: Hodder and Stoughton, 2007, p. 239.

258. Dillon, *Dirty War*, pp. xix, 45-46, 51-55; Taylor, *Brits*, pp. 128-137; Peter Carrington (Defence Secretary) to Edward Heath (Prime Minister), *Special Reconnaissance Unit*, November 28, 1972, DEFE25/282(NAUK); Faligot, *Kitson Experiment*.

259. Raymond Murray, *The SAS in Ireland*, Cork, Ireland: Mercier Press, 1990. On the decision to deploy 22SAS, see MISC115(76)1st meeting, *Cabinet Committee on Northern Ireland*, January 6, 1976, CAB130, No. 908(NAUK); Memorandum by Fred Mulley (Defence Secretary) and Roy Mason (Northern Ireland Secretary) to James Callaghan (Prime Minister), December 3, 1976, PREM16/1342(NAUK).

260. Frank Bovenkerk and Yucel Yesilgoz, *The Turkish Mafia*, Preston, UK: Milo Books, 2007, pp. 185, 197-198, 204-208, 214-216, 227, 231-232; Gareth Jenkins, "Susurluk and the Legacy of Turkey's Dirty War," *Jamestown Foundation Terrorism Monitor*, Vol. 6, No. 9, May 1, 2008; Bill Park, "Turkey's Deep State: Ergenekon and the Threat to Democratisation in the Republic," *RUSI Journal*, Vol. 153, No. 5, 2008, pp. 54-59; "Turkey general denies coup plot," BBC News, January 26, 2010, available from *news.bbc.co.uk/go/pr/fr/-/1/hi/world/europe/8480028.stm*.

261. For a prime example of a source tainted by conspiracy theorizing, see Daniele Ganser, *NATO's Secret Armies; Operation Gladio and Terrorism in Western Europe*, Frank Cass, 2005. As Leopoldo Nuti and Olav Riste delicately comment, Ganser's "ambitious conclusions do not seem to be entirely corroborated by a sound examination of the sources available." "Introduction—Strategy of 'Stay-Behind'," *Journal of Strategic Studies*, Vol. 30, No. 6, 2007, p. 930. This edition of the *Journal* is recommended reading for any scholar interested in the "stay-behind" networks established in Western Europe during the early Cold War period.

262. "A Trip Through the Borderlands," *The Economist*, March 13, 2010; Jack Barclay, "Collateral damage; Propaganda defends Muslim casualties," *JIR*, Vol. 22, No. 5 (201), pp. 20-25.

263. "Unleashing the Laws of War," *The Economist*, August 15, 2009.

264. Interview with General Larry Arnold (USAF) by 9/11 Commission, February 3, 2004, available from *media.nara.gov/ 9-11/MFR/t-0148-911MFR-00172.pdf*; Statement of General Ralph E. Eberhart (USAF), CINC NORAD, to U.S. Senate Armed Services Committee, March 20, 2002, available from *armed-services.senate.gov/statemnt/2002/March/Eberhart.pdf*; Julian Borger, "US Civilian Planes 'Shot Down' Four Times a Week in Post-September 11 Drills," *The Guardian*, October 4, 2003. NORAD is a bi-national military command, with a U.S. Air Force chief and a deputy from the Canadian Forces. The combined character of NORAD is often forgotten, particularly by cranks who claim that it was deliberately "stood down" by the Bush administration on the morning of 9/11.

265. In response to this dilemma, the Federal Constitutional Court of Germany has ruled that it is illegal for the *Luftwaffe* to shoot down hijacked jets. Ulf Gartzke, "Flying Blind in the Post-9/11 World," *The Weekly Standard*, February 3, 2006, available from *www.weeklystandard.com/Content/Public/Articles/000%5C000 %5C011%5C933pgtee.asp*.

266. BGS(Int)1/16, *Historical Narrative of Interrogation*, November 21, 1971, DEFE23/109(NAUK); Hennessey, *Troubles*, pp. 129-167, 214-226; Benest, "Northern Ireland," pp. 136-137; Dixon, "Northern Ireland," pp. 448, 457. New guidelines on interrogation and detainee handling did not stop further allegations of physical ill-treatment described by the European Court of Human Rights as "inhuman and degrading treatment" in 1978. See Brice Dickson, "Counter-Insurgency and Human Rights in Northern Ireland," *The Journal of Strategic Studies*, Vol. 32, No. 3, 2009, p. 487.

267. Josh White, "Military Lawyers Fought Policy on Interrogations," *The Washington Post*, July 15, 2005; Memorandum by Secretary of Defense Donald Rumsfeld, *Counter-Resistance Techniques in the War on Terrorism*, April 16, 2003, available from *www.humanrightsfirst.org/us_law/etn/gonzales/memos_dir/mem_*

20030416_Rum_IntTec.pdf; JAG memos, introduced into Congressional Record by Senator Lindsey Graham (R-SC), July 25, 2005, available from *www.humanrightsfirst.org/us_law/etn/ pdf/ jag-memos-072505.pdf*.

268. "The Dark Pursuit of the Truth," *The Economist*, August 1, 2009. Detainee abuses in Afghanistan are the subject of the documentary *Taxi to the Dark Side* (2007).

269. Taylor, "Six Days that Shook Britain."

270. Taylor, "Six Days that Shook Britain;" Urban, *Big Boys' Rules*, pp. 140, 171; Report by Captain A. C. Massey (22SAS), *Comments on the Tactical Aspects of the Handling of the "Munich Massacre,"* September 18, 1972, in GEN129(72)3, *The Munich Incident*, October 12, 1972, CAB130/616(NAUK).

271. Taylor, *Brits*, pp. 270-277; Harnden, *Bandit Country*, pp. 418-423. In military parlance, an "ambush" is an operation to take an enemy force by surprise and destroy it with maximum use of firepower. With a preemptive intervention, the intention is to try and arrest the terrorist (or terrorists), although lethal force may be required for self-defense.

272. Tony Geraghty, *Who Dares Wins: The Story of the SAS 1950-1992*, London, UK: Little, Brown & Co, 1992, pp. 232-234, 247-252; Dillon, *Dirty War*, pp. 465-478.

273. Ian Jack, "Gibraltar," in *The Best of Granta Reportage*, London, UK: Penguin, 1994, pp. 187-255; Urban, *Big Boys' Rules*, p. 205; Taylor, *Brits*, pp. 283-284. The two corporals were not members of 22SAS or 14 Intelligence Company, and their presence at the funeral is unexplained. Mourners evidently suspected that a repeat of Stone's attack was imminent and reacted by beating and shooting the two soldiers.

274. Taylor, *Brits*, p. 309; B'Tselem Report, *Activity of the Undercover Units in the Occupied Territories*, Jerusalem, Israel: May 1992; Cronin, *How Terrorism Ends*, pp. 30-31; Rotem Giladi, "Out of Context: 'Undercover' Operations and [International Humanitarian Law] Advocacy in the Occupied Palestinian Territories," *Journal of Conflict & Security Law*, Vol. 14, No. 3, 2010, pp. 393-439.

275. Jones, "Israel," p. 275; Cronin, *How Terrorism Ends*, p. 53; Mohammed Hafez and Joseph Hatfeld, "Do Targeted Assassinations Work? A Multivariate Analysis of Israel's Controversial Tactic during the Al-Aqsa Uprising," *SC&T*, Vol. 29, No. 4, 2006, pp. 359-382; Jones, "al-Aqsa intifada," p. 134.

276. Taylor, *Brits*, pp. 1, 302; Iron, "Longest War," pp. 177-178; Moloney, *IRA*, pp. 332-33, 335-336, 458-459. Based on this evidence, the author does not subscribe to Brice Dickson's argument that agent recruitment was of little practical utility, although he agrees with his assessments on its ethical and legal implications. See Dickson, "Counter-Insurgency and Human Rights," pp. 475-493.

277. John Ware, "Torture, Murder, Mayhem, the Dirty War Just Got Dirtier," *The Guardian*, May 12, 2003; Matthew Teague, "Double Blind," *The Atlantic Monthly*, April 2006, available from *www.theatlantic.com/doc/print/200604/ ira-spy*.

278. Lewis, *Fishers of Men*, p. 236; Ingram and Harkin, *Stakeknife*; Bamford, "Intelligence," pp. 592-593, 600-603; Hoffman, *Inside Terrorism*, p. 271. For a balanced analysis of the ethical and practical problems of agent recruitment, see Jon Moran, "Evaluating Special Branch and the Use of Informant Intelligence in Northern Ireland," *Intelligence and National Security*, Vol. 25, No. 1, 2010, pp. 1-23.

279. Carlos Osorio, ed., "Bordaberry Condemned for 1973 Coup," *National Security Archive Electronic Briefing Book* No. 309, March 20, 2010, available from *www.gwu.edu/-nsarchiv/NSAEBB/NSAEBB309/*.

280. Thomas Marks and David Scott Palmer, "Radical Maoist Insurgents and Terrorist Tactics: Comparing Nepal and Peru," *Low Intensity Conflict & Law Enforcement,* Vol. 13, No. 2, 2005, pp. 107-108; Jo-Marie Burt, "Playing Politics with Terror: The Case of Fujimori's Peru," in Kassimeris, ed., *Playing Politics*, pp. 62-100; Cronin, *How Terrorism Ends*, pp. 125-131.

281. Lewis, *Guerrillas and Generals*; Richard Gillespie, "Political Violence in Argentina: Guerrillas, Terrorists and *Carapintadas*," in Crenshaw, *Terrorism in Context*, pp. 211-248; Videla is quoted on p. 243.

282. Dmitry Gorenburg, "Russia Confronts Radical Islam," *Current History*, Vol. 105, No. 693, 2006, pp. 334-340; Charles King, "Prisoners of the Caucasus: Russia's Invisible Civil War," *Foreign Affairs*, Vol. 89, No. 4, 2010, pp. 20-34.

283. "Violence continues in Russian North Caucasus," *Jane's Intelligence Weekly*, August 19, 2009; Mairbek Vatchagaev, "More Russian Troops Headed to Ingushetia," *Jamestown Foundation Eurasia Daily Monitor*, Vol. 6, No. 162, August 21, 2009; Unnamed author, "Northern Explosion—Violence Escalates in the North Caucasus," *JIR*, Vol. 21, No. 10, 2009, pp. 8-13.

284. Rhys Blakely, "Tamil death toll 'is 1,400 a week' at Manik Farm camp in Sri Lanka," *The Times*, June 10 2009; Andrew Buncombe, "Up to 40,000 Civilians 'Died in Sri Lanka Offensive'," *The Independent*, February 10, 2010; Nira Wickramasinghe, "In Sri Lanka, the Triumph of Vulgar Patriotism," *Current History*, Vol. 109, No. 726, 2010, pp. 158-161.

285. "Behind the Rajapaksa Brothers' Smiles," *The Economist*, August 8, 2009. This article's title refers to both the President and his brother, Defence Secretary Gotabhaya Rajapaksa. Andrew Buncombe, "Wife's Fears of General Imprisoned in Sri Lanka," *The Independent*, February 10, 2010.

286. Pressman, "Power without Influence," p. 174; Bruce Hoffman, "A Counterterrorism Strategy for the Obama Administration," *Terrorism and Political Violence*, Vol. 21, No. 3, 2009, pp. 360-361.

287. Speech by Secretary Robert Gates to National Defense University, September 29, 2008, emphasis added, available from *www.defenselink.mil/speeches/speech.aspx?speechid=1279*.

288. Chin, "War on Terror"; Hew Strachan, "The Strategic Gap in British Defence Policy," *Survival*, Vol. 51, No. 4, 2009, pp. 49-70.

289. Claire Taylor and Jon Lunn, *Strategic Defence and Security Review*, London, UK: House of Commons Library, August 16, 2010; Speech by Liam Fox (Defence Secretary) at Royal Institute for Chartered Surveyors on August 13, 2010, available

from *www.mod.uk/DefenceInternet/AboutDefence/People/Speeches/ SofS/20100813/TheNeedForDefenceReform.htm.*

290. Hew Strachan, "The Lost Meaning of Strategy," *Survival*, Vol. 47, No. 3, 2005, pp. 33-54.

291. Roland D. Crelinstein and Alex P. Schmid, "Western Responses to Terrorism: A Twenty-Five Year Balance Sheet," *Terrorism and Political Violence*, Vol. 4, No. 4, 1992, p. 335.

292. Strachan, "Making Strategy," pp. 66-67.

293. Moloney, *IRA*, pp. 304-319, 368-371; Iron, "Longest War," pp. 183-184.

294. Eric Schmitt and Scott Shane, "Crux of Afghan Debate: Will More Troops Curb Terror?" *New York Times*, September 8, 2009; Austin Long, "Small is Beautiful: The Counterterrorism Option in Afghanistan," *Orbis*, Vol. 54, No. 2, 2010, pp. 199-214.

295. Boyle, "Do counterterrorism and counterinsurgency go together," p. 335.

296. *Ibid.*; Max Boot, "How We Can Win in Afghanistan," *Commentary*, November, 2009, available from *www.commentarymagazine.com/viewarticle.cfm,/how-we-can-win-in-afghanistan-15257.*

297. Rashid, *Descent into Chaos*, p. 106; The reliability of local proxies is also referred to in "Afghan warlord 'paid $2m' by UK," BBC News, January 9, 2010, available from *news.bbc.co.uk/go,/pr/ fr -/1/hi/uk/8448825.stm*, with reference to an anti-Taliban militia hired by the SIS during the initial phases of Operation ENDURING FREEDOM, who subsequently allowed al-Qaeda fighters to escape (for a fee) during the battle of Tora Bora in December 2001. The author is reminded of the cynical adage that "you cannot buy an Afghan—you may only rent him." Synnott, *Transforming Pakistan*, p. 116.

298. Boyle, "Do counterterrorism and counterinsurgency go together," pp. 350-351; Kilcullen, *Accidental Guerrilla*, pp. 34-38, 287-289.

299. Matthew B; Arnold, "The US 'Surge' as a Collaborative Corrective for Iraq," *RUSI Journal*, Vol. 153, No. 2, 2008, pp. 24-29; Boot, "How We Can Win"; Sloggett, "Attack of the drones," p. 15.

300. Dimitrakis, "Cyprus Insurgency," p. 389; Richard Aldrich, *The Hidden Hand: Britain, America and Cold War Secret Intelligence*, London, UK: John Murray, 2001, p. 578.

301. Robert Kaplan, "Buddha's Savage Peace," *The Atlantic*, September, 2009; Anthony Loyd, "New Tamil group People's Liberation Army vows to start a fresh war," *The Times*, December 7, 2009; *Joint Humanitarian Update 10-23 April, 2010*, New York: UN Office for the Co-ordination of Humanitarian Affairs, April 29, 2010.

302. Cronin, *How Terrorism Ends*, p. 11.

303. "Text: Beirut Declaration," BBC News, March 28, 2002, available from *news.bbc.co.uk/1/hi/world/monitoring/media_reports/1899395.stm*; "Not Quite as Gloomy as They Look," *The Economist*, August 1, 2009.

304. Austin Long, "The Anbar Awakening," *Survival*, Vol. 50, No. 2, 2008, pp. 67-94; Lawrence Wright, "The Rebellion Within: an Al-Qaeda Mastermind Questions Terrorism," *New Yorker*, June 2, 2008; Peter Bergen and Paul Cruickshank, "The Unraveling: The Jihadist Revolt against bin Laden," *New Republic*, June 11, 2008; Porter, "Long wars," p. 303; Boyle, "Do counterterrorism and counterinsurgency go together," p. 338.

305. Cronin, *Ending Terrorism*, p. 27. A copy of Zawahiri's letter—which was recovered by the U.S. military in Iraq—is available from *www.globalsecurity.org/security/library/report/2005/ zawahiri-zarqawi-letter_9jul2005.htm*; Barak Mendelsohn, "Al-Qaeda's Palestinian Problem," *Survival*, Vol. 51, No. 4, 2009, pp. 71-86. In a recent poll surveying Arab opinion on Palestine, 38 percent of those polled stated that the issue was the "most important" for the Arab world, 38 percent stated it was within "the top three priorities," 23 percent stated it was within "the top five" of priorities, and only 1 percent declared it to be "unimportant." See "Waking From Its Sleep: A Special Report on the Arab World," *The Economist*, July 25, 2009.

306. Cronin, *Ending Terrorism*, p. 11; Colin McInnes and Caroline Kennedy-Pipe, "The British Army and the Peace Process in Ireland," *The Journal of Conflict Studies*, Vol. 21, No. 1, 2001, pp. 21-45. See also the article "Dying Spasms," The Economist, August 8, 2009.

307. Kilcullen, *Accidental Guerrilla*, pp. 12-13; Porter, "Long Wars," pp. 296-305.

308. Gompert, "Underkill," pp. 159-174.

309. Tim Weinert, *Legacy of Ashes; The History of the CIA*, London, UK: Penguin, 2008, pp. 539-561; Amy Zegart, "9/11 and the FBI: The Organizational Roots of Failure," *Intelligence & National Security*, Vol. 22, No. 2, 2007, pp. 165-184.

310. James Hider, "'Orchard of fighters' grows out of poverty"; and "Yemen forces shoot al-Qaeda militants as country nears ruin," *The Times*, January 4, 2010; Ginny Hill, "What is Happening in Yemen," *Survival*, Vol. 52, No. 2, 2010, pp. 105-116.

311. Mukhtar A. Khan, "Pakistani Government Offensive in Swat Heading for the Taliban of Waziristan," *JFTM*, Vol. 12, No. 17, June 18, 2009.

312. Stephen Cohen, "How a Botched US Alliance Fed Pakistan's Crisis," *Current History*, Vol. 109, No. 726, 2010, pp. 138-143.

313. Hennessey, *Troubles*.

314. Sean Rayment, "Britain unprepared for Mumbai-style attack, former head of SAS says," *Daily Telegraph*, November 29, 2008; Kim Sengupta, "Fear of Mumbai-style Attack Prompts UK Security Review," *The Independent*, December 3, 2008; "UK's National Security Strategy Needs Radical Change, says Independent All-Party Commission of Experts at IPPR," London, UK: Institute for Public Policy Research, June 30, 2009, available from *www.ippr. org.uk/security/pressreleases.asp?id=3626&tID=2656.*

GLOSSARY AND ABBREVIATIONS

22SAS   22nd Special Air Service Regiment.

Action Directe   A French far-left terrorist group active during the 1980s.

Auto-golpe   "Auto-coup." The term given to Peruvian President Alberto Fujimori's assumption of authoritarian power in April 1992.

AFRICOM   Africa Command. The U.S. military's regional command covering all of Africa (bar Egypt, which is still within Central Command's area of operations).

AFP   Armed Forces of the Philippines.

AKP   *Adelet ve Kalkinma Partisi.* A Turkish Political Party.

al-Qaeda   Translates from Arabic as "the base" or "the foundation." Originally founded by Osama bin Laden in the latter phases of the anti-Soviet jihad in Afghanistan, al-Qaeda is now considered by scholars of terrorism to consist of a network of groups or individuals drawn together by the movements' common hostility to Western governments, Israel and "apostate" regimes in the Islamic world and to share the long-term goal of founding a global caliphate.

ANC	African National Congress.
ANO	Abu Nidal Organisation. A defunct Palestinian terrorist group led by Sabri el-Banna ("Abu Nidal"). El-Banna died in mysterious circumstances in Baghdad on August 16, 2002, either as a result of suicide or execution by the Baathist regime.
ANP	Afghan National Police.
AQAP	Al-Qaeda in the Arabian Peninsula.
AQI	Al-Qaeda in Iraq.
AQIM	Al-Qaeda in the Islamic Maghreb.
BBE	*Bijzondere Bijstands Eenheid.* Dutch counterterrorist unit formed from the Royal Netherlands Marine Corps.
BR	*Brigate Rosse.* Italian Red Brigades.
BSF	The Indian Border Security Force.
BSO	Black September Organization. A terrorist network set up after

the PLO's expulsion from Jordan (July 1971) to conduct deniable attacks on behalf of Fatah. The organization took its name from the month in which King Hussein unleashed the Jordanian army against Palestinian *fedayeen* based in his country (September 1970).

B Specials — The Northern Ireland police reserve force disbanded by the British in January 1970.

Bundeswehr — The Federal German armed forces.

CALABA — Code name given to the British Army's methods of "deep interrogation," applied to some Republican terrorist suspects in Northern Ireland during the early 1970s. The methods (which included sensory deprivation techniques such as "hooding" suspects and subjecting them to "white noise" prior to interrogation) were abandoned after they were condemned by the European Commission on Human Rights in September 1972.

CBRN — Chemical, Biological, Radiological and Nuclear.

CCRF — Civil Contingencies Reaction Force.

Carabinieri	Italian paramilitary police.
CENTCOM	U.S. Central Command.
CGS	Chief of the General Staff (UK).
CIA	Central Intelligence Agency.
CJTF-HOA	Combined Joint Task Force-Horn of Africa. According to NATO terminology, a "joint" force incorporates elements from more than one of the three armed services (Navy, Army, Air Force) while a "combined" force includes military units from more than one country (see CTF below). A CJTF is therefore comprised of the maritime, land, and/or air forces drawn from a coalition of states.
COBRA	Cabinet Office Briefing Room "A." Established in late 1972, this is the British government's principal deliberative body in the event of a crisis arising from terrorism or other significant emergencies. It is named after the room within the Cabinet Offices where this body meets.
COIN	Common acronym for COunter-INsurgency.
CONTEST	Official acronym for the UK government's COuNterTerrorism STrategy.

CTF	Combined Task Force. U.S. and NATO term for a multinational military formation drawn from similar services (in the case of CTF150, from the navies of several countries).
Dietrologia	An Italian term that loosely translates as "behind-ology." This phrase describes the popularity of conspiracy theories in Italy.
Delta Force	A U.S. Army special forces unit, specifically established for counterterrorism.
Derin Devlet	Turkish for "deep state." A term given to the clique of military and security force officers (and their civilian sympathisers) which allegedly constitutes the real power behind the government in Ankara.
DFLP	Democratic Front for the Liberation of Palestine.
Echelon	An Anglo-American intelligence-sharing program incorporating GCHQ and NSA (see below), that also includes its Australian, Canadian, and New Zealand counterparts.
EOKA	"National Organisation of Cypriot Fighters." The Greek Cypriot

terrorist group fighting British rule from 1955-1959.

Ergenekon The name given to an alleged plot organized by officials within the "deep state" to overthrow the AKP government in Turkey. The Ergenekon scandal has polarised Turkish politics since 86 suspected plotters were put on trial in October 2008.

ETA *Euzkadi to Askatasuna.* Basque terrorist group fighting for independence from Spain.

FARC Revolutionary Armed Forces of Colombia.

FATA The Federally Administered Tribal Areas of Pakistan. The FATA consists of seven agencies (Bajaur, Mohmand, Khyber, Orakzai, Kurram, North Waziristan, and South Waziristan).

Fatah The Palestinian nationalist movement, formerly a terrorist organization, now officially committed to achieving a peace settlement with Israel. Not to be confused with FATA.

FBI Federal Bureau of Investigation.

FCO	Foreign and Commonwealth Office.
FLN	Algerian National Liberation Front.
FLQ	*Front de Liberation du Quebec.* A terrorist group briefly engaged in 1970 in a campaign for the independence of Francophone Quebec from Canada.
FRG	Federal Republic of Germany.
FRU	Force Research Unit. A controversial British Army intelligence formation that recruited agents within Republican and Loyalist organizations in Northern Ireland during the 1980s-1990s.
FSB	*Federalnaya Sluzhba Byezopasnosti.* Federal Security Service. The internal security service of the Russian Federation.
Garda Siochana	Police service of the Republic of Ireland.
GCHQ	Government Communications Headquarters. The UK's SIGINT service.
GDR	German Democratic Republic.

GHQ	General Headquarters.
GIA	*Groupe Islamiste Armée.* A radical Islamist group involved in the Algerian Civil War (1992-2002).
GIGN	*Groupe d'Intervention de Gendarmerie Nationale.* French counterterrorist unit raised from France's *Gendarmerie Nationale.*
GOC	General Officer Commanding.
GSG9	*Grenzschutzgruppe-Neun.* A German counterterrorist unit raised from the *Bundespolizei* (formerly known as the *Bundesgrenzschutz*).
GSPC	*Groupe Salafiste pour la Prédication et de Combat.* A sister movement to the GIA, now part of AQIM.
Hamas	The principal Palestinian Islamist movement, affiliated with the Muslim Brotherhood.
Hezbollah	"Party of God." A hybrid political-military movement with its core support based within Lebanon's Shia community.
HRW	Human Rights Watch.
HUM	*Harkat ul-Mujahidin.* Pakistani Islamist group involved in fighting

the Kashmir insurgency. Known as Harkat ul-Ansar before 1998.

HUMINT	Human Intelligence. In this context, information gained from clandestine surveillance, informants within the civilian community, and agents recruited within a terrorist group.
ICU	Islamic Courts Union. The Islamist government of Somalia from May to December 2006.
IDF	Israeli Defense Force.
IMU	Islamic Movement of Uzbekistan.
INLA	Irish National Liberation Army.
INS	Irish Naval Service.
IPS	Iraqi Police Service.
IR	Islamic Resistance. The guerrilla/terrorist wing of Hezbollah.
ISA	Intelligence Support Activity. A U.S. Army unit formed in January 1981 to conduct clandestine intelligence gathering. ISA is still in service, although it has undergone numerous changes of name since the late-1980s.

ISAF	International Security Assistance Force, Afghanistan. The NATO-led security mission in Afghanistan.
ISI	Pakistani Inter-Services Intelligence organization.
JAG	Judge Advocate Generals Corps. (U.S.)
Jandarma	The Turkish gendarmerie.
JCS	Joint Chiefs of Staff.
Jemaah Islamiyah	The Southeast Asian branch of al-Qaeda.
JITEM	*Jandarme İstihbarat ve Terörle Mücadele Merkezi.* A covert counterterrorist force of the jandarma, currently accused of human rights abuses in the war against the PKK, and also organized criminal activity.
Knesset	The Israeli parliament.
KRG	Kurdish Regional Government. Based in Irbil, Northern Iraq.
LET	*Lashkar e-Toiba.* A Pakistani Islamist group active in the Kashmir insurgency, responsible for the Mumbai massacre (November 2008).

LOAC	Laws of Armed Conflict.
Loyalist	In the context of Northern Ireland, this was the term applied to members of the Protestant community whose commitment to the Unionist cause was such that they were prepared to resort to terrorism against the local Catholic community.
LTTE	The Liberation Tigers of Tamil Eelam, commonly known as the "Tamil Tigers."
MACA	Military Aid to the Civil Authority. Official British government term for the call-up of the armed forces to assist in a domestic emergency.
MACC	Military Aid to the Civil Community. Official British government term for the employment of the armed forces for disaster relief.
MACP	Military Aid to the Civil Power. Official British government term given to the use of the Army to preserve domestic law and order.
MI5	The UK's internal security service.
Ministerium fur Staatssicherheit	The former East German secret police.

Mkhonto we Sizwe	"Spear of the Nation." The military wing of the African National Congress (until its incorporation into the South African National Defence Force in 1994).
MNF	The Multinational Force (consisting of U.S., French, Italian, and British units) sent to Lebanon in 1983.
MOD	UK Ministry of Defence.
Mossad	Hebrew for "the Institute." The Israeli foreign intelligence service.
MRF	Military Reaction Force (also dubbed in secondary literature as the "Mobile Reconnaissance Force"). A controversial plainclothes British Army intelligence unit active in Belfast in 1971-72. The MRF was subsequently replaced by 14 Intelligence Company, the precursor to the SRR (see below).
MVD	*Ministerstvo Vnutrennikh Dyel.* Russian Ministry of Internal Affairs. The MVD has its own military arm known as the *vnutrenniye voiska* ("interior troops').
NATO	North Atlantic Treaty Organization.

NGO	Non-Governmental Organization.
NIO	Northern Ireland Office.
NORAD	North American Air Defense Command. A combined organization incorporating the U.S. Air Force and the Canadian Forces, responsible for protecting North American airspace.
N17	"The Revolutionary Organisation 17th November." A far-left Greek terrorist group.
NSA	National Security Agency. The U.S. SIGINT service.
NSC	National Security Council (U.S.).
NSG	National Security Guard. An elite Indian counterterrorist unit.
NWFP	The Northwest Frontier Province of Pakistan.
OHD	*Ozel Harp Dairesi.* "Special Warfare Group." A clandestine branch of the Turkish Army founded in 1952 to organize resistance in the event of a Soviet invasion.
PFLP	Popular Front for the Liberation of Palestine. A rival to Fatah, and one of the first major terrorist groups to hijack airliners.

PIJ	Palestinian Islamic Jihad.
PIRA	Provisional Irish Republican Army. The Provisional IRA split from the Official IRA in January 1970, emerging as the principal Republican group fighting for a united Ireland.
PKK	Kurdistan Worker's Party *(Partiya Karkeren Kurdistan)*. A terrorist/insurgent group fighting for Kurdish independence from Turkey.
PLF	Palestine Liberation Front. A minor group responsible for the *Achille Lauro* hijacking in October 1985.
PLO	Palestine Liberation Organisation. The umbrella group led by Fatah from 1969, campaigning by diplomatic and military means for the Palestinian cause.
QRA	Quick Reaction Alert force. An RAF squadron assigned in the aftermath of September 11, 2001 (9/11), to be on stand-by to react to a aerial hijacking in British airspace.
RAF	Royal Air Force.

Republicanism	In an Irish context, the name given to the ideology within Northern Ireland and Eire that favors and end to British rule over the Northern six counties of Ireland and their reunification with the Irish Republic.
ROE	Rules of Engagement. Regulations governing the military's use of lethal force.
RR	Rashtriya Rifles. An Indian paramilitary force raised specifically for COIN in Kashmir.
RUC	Royal Ulster Constabulary. Renamed the Police Service of Northern Ireland on April 4, 2001.
Sayeret Maktal	Israeli army special forces.
SB	Special Branch. Term given to the branch of a British police force assigned to counterterrorism.
SBS	Special Boat Service. The special forces unit of the Royal Marines.
SCO	Shanghai Cooperation Organization.
SDLP	Social Democratic and Labour Party. A moderate Nationalist political party in Northern Ireland,

committed to the goal of a united Ireland through constitutional, nonviolent means.

SDSR	Strategic Defence and Security Review (UK).
Sendero Luminoso	"Shining Path." A Maoist insurgent/terrorist group active in Peru from May 1980. It is still active, although far from its peak strength during the late 1980s.
Sepah e-Pasdaran	The Iranian Revolutionary Guard Corps.
Shayetet 13	The Israeli Navy's special forces.
Shin Bet	The Israeli internal security service.
SID	Military Intelligence Service (Italy).
SIGINT	Signals Intelligence.
Sinn Fein	"Ourselves Alone." The principal political party within the Irish Republican movement, hitherto the political spokesmen of PIRA.
SIS	Secret Intelligence Service. The UK's external intelligence service.
Spetsnaz	Term given to Russian military and security services special forces. An abbreviation of "spet-

sialnovo naznachenia' ("special designation").

Solidarnosc	"Solidarity." An independent trade union formed in Communist-era Poland in 1980, which was subsequently involved in a nonviolent campaign for civil liberties and multiparty democracy.
SRR	Special Reconnaissance Regiment. A British Army unit established in April 2005 for clandestine surveillance.
Taliban	A Sunni Islamist movement (named after the Pashto phrase for "madrassah students") that governed Afghanistan from September 1996 to November 2001, and is currently waging an insurgency against the NATO-backed government in Kabul.
TFG	The Transitional Federal Government of Somalia.
TTP	Tehrik e-Taleban Pakistan. The alliance of Taliban-affiliated tribes and foreign militants currently fighting an insurgency in the NWFP and FATA.
UAE	United Arab Emirates.

UAV	Unmanned Aerial Vehicle.
UDR	Ulster Defence Regiment. Formed in January 1970 to supplement the regular British Army in counterterrorist operations. The UDR was amalgamated with the Royal Irish Regiment following the UK Defence Review of 1991.
Unionism	The name given to political opinion within Northern Ireland (within the Protestant majority) that supports Northern Ireland's constitutional status as part of the UK.
UNSC	United Nations Security Council.
WMD	Weapons of Mass Destruction. Popular term given to CBRN weapons.

MILITARY OPERATIONS CITED IN THE TEXT

ACTIVE ENDEAVOUR	NATO maritime counterterrorist patrols in the Mediterranean.
BANNER	The British Army's MACP mission in Northern Ireland from 1969-2007.
BLUE STAR	The Indian Army operation to recapture the Golden Temple in Amritsar (June 3-6, 1984).
CAST LEAD	The IDF incursion into Gaza in December 2008-January 2009.
EAGLE CLAW	The abortive U.S. military attempt to free the embassy hostages in Iran, April 1980.
EL DORADO CANYON	U.S. air-strikes against Libya in April 1986.
ENDURING FREEDOM	The U.S. military name for counterterrorist and COIN operations in Afghanistan since October 2001.
FLAVIUS	An operation mounted by the Gibraltar police, MI5, and 22SAS to arrest three PIRA terrorists planning a bombing attack in this crown colony (March 6, 1988).

FLINTLOCK	A multinational exercise in Northwest Africa, May 2010.
INFINITE REACH	The U.S. cruise missile strikes on Afghanistan and Sudan in August 1998.
IRAQI FREEDOM	The U.S. military term for the invasion and occupation of Iraq (March 2003 onward).
JACANA	The multilateral military operation to clear al-Qaeda in Southeastern Afghanistan after Operation ANACONDA (March 2002).
MARMION	A British contingency plan from the early 1970s, outlining the deployment of troops to Heathrow Airport in response to intelligence of a precise terrorist threat.
MONOGRAM	A UK MOD program for training overseas militaries in counterterrorism and COIN.
NIMROD	The storming of the Iranian embassy in London by 22SAS on May 5, 1980.
SUN	The Turkish military incursion into Northern Iraq in February 2008.